SEWN *By* HAND

SEWN *By* HAND

TWO DOZEN PROJECTS
STITCHED WITH NEEDLE & THREAD

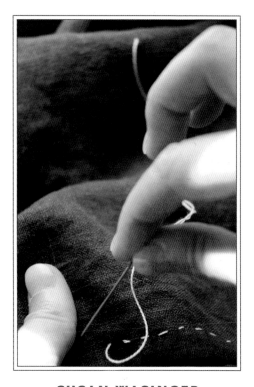

SUSAN WASINGER

LARK CRAFTS

An Imprint of Sterling Publishing Co., Inc.
New York

WWW.LARKCRAFTS.COM

Library of Congress Cataloging-in-Publication Data

Wasinger, Susan.
  Sewn by hand : two dozen projects stitched with needle & thread / Susan Wasinger. -- 1st ed.
      p. cm.
  Includes bibliographical references and index.
  ISBN 978-1-60059-668-1 (alk. paper)
  1. Textile crafts. 2. Needlework. I. Title.
  TT699.W388 2011
  746.4--dc22

                                        2010037698

10 9 8 7 6 5 4 3 2 1

First Edition

Published by Lark Crafts
An Imprint of Sterling Publishing Co., Inc.
387 Park Avenue South, New York, NY 10016

Text, Photography, and Illustration © 2011, Susan Wasinger

Distributed in Canada by Sterling Publishing,
c/o Canadian Manda Group, 165 Dufferin Street
Toronto, Ontario, Canada M6K 3H6

Distributed in the United Kingdom by GMC Distribution Services,
Castle Place, 166 High Street, Lewes, East Sussex, England BN7 1XU

Distributed in Australia by Capricorn Link (Australia) Pty Ltd.,
P.O. Box 704, Windsor, NSW 2756 Australia

If you have questions or comments about this book, please contact:
Lark Crafts
67 Broadway
Asheville, NC 28801
828-253-0467

Manufactured in China

ISBN 13: 978-1-60059-668-1

For information about custom editions, special sales, premium and corporate purchases, please contact Sterling Special Sales Department at 800-805-5489 or specialsales@sterlingpub.com.

For information about desk and examination copies available to college and university professors, requests must be submitted to academic@larkbooks.com. Our complete policy can be found at www.larkcrafts.com.

Senior Editor:
VALERIE VAN ARSDALE SHRADER

**Design, Photography,
and Illustration:**
SUSAN WASINGER

Assistant Editor:
THOM O'HEARN

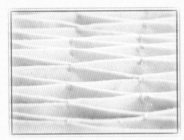  

ESSENTIAL TOOLS & USEFUL THOUGHTS

Hand-Sewn PROJECTS

SOULFUL STITCHING

There are so many words that speak to the power and grace of our hands.

For example, flattering and positive adjectives like "handy" for something practical and "handsome" for something beautiful. There are also words that incorporate the Latin word for hand, like "manifest" for the incarnation of an abstract idea. This whole hand sewing thing started for me as a concept, kind of an, "hhhmmm, I wonder..."

I wonder what a pair of hands, armed with nothing but a needle and thread, can accomplish. I believe this little seed of a question was planted in my head by my restless hands. Hands that were tired of the tyranny of machines, the indifferent touch of the keyboard and the mouse. Hands that wanted to be of use, from fingertip to palm, for some purpose higher than typing another email or white-knuckling the steering wheel through rush-hour traffic. That is how it started at least. Innocent enough...but then I picked up that thread, prodded a little piece of linen with my needle, and out popped one intriguing little project—which turned into five, and five into twenty, and so on and so on.

And before long, it wasn't just a project, it was a revelation.

Stitching by hand has opened up a world of soulful sewing pleasure that was never a part of the craft when I was chained to my sewing machine in a room all by myself. There is a tenderness and simplicity to dipping the needle gently in and out of the fabric, a real tactile sweetness to it. It is much nicer than trying to steer a speeding, careening machine—with needle pumping and presser foot thumping—down an unwieldy seam. And did I mention how nice it is to be able to sit with my family at the kitchen table, kids working on homework, husband playing the guitar, actually making lovely and useful things? And the stitching can continue on my daughter's soccer sidelines, in front of Jane Austen movies, hanging out with friends at cafés, in the car waiting to pick up my son, and on the deck, looking at mountains on a sunny, summer day. But it is not just that portability, or the fact that you can pick it up and put it down any old time, there is one more awe-inspiring, life-changing thing about stitching by hand:

THE SILENCE.

It is breathtaking. Hand sewing has made me realize how very little silence we ever have these days. Most of the time we are on the phone, or watching something on a screen, or listening to the news, or nagging our children, or just being bombarded by various whirrings, spinnings, buzzings, and ringings ricocheting toward us from every angle. But here is a comfortable, cheerful, engaged, and productive silence. While hand sewing, you are focused on this one quiet task, and your mind quiets down, too. Your hands are happy to be positively engaged and relishing their powerful ability to bring something new to life. It is an almost ridiculously cheerful silence.

And when you are done with silence, hand stitching won't get in your way. No one can talk to you over the hum of a sewing machine, but the progress of a needle and thread is as silent as fog and sallies forth on little cat feet.

One tiny stitch at a time turns out to be a very comfortable human pace. Do I sound like I am a hundred years old? Maybe, but what I have discovered is that there is an infinite supply of charm inherent in the tiny, tidy, even puckers of the hand-stitched seam. Nowadays, I am letting the stitches show wherever possible. And those stitches just keep suggesting more projects. Hand sewing connects you with each stitch and slows you down just enough that you find yourself enjoying the process. I am finding that hand sewing is a bit like taking the two-lane highways instead of the interstate. It's a little slower, but the character, charm, and unique soulfulness of those back roads is priceless and precious beyond hours. So each hand-sewn project is like that journey, taken one stitch at a time...Why don't you come along?

ESSENTIAL HAND SEWING TOOLS

Here's what you need again and again in your hand sewing basket. It's not an extensive list, and once you have cut out your materials or finished a tricky part, you may want to use the little portable sewing pouch on page 80 to take it with you on the road.

SCISSORS You'll want three different kinds of scissors: a pair of dressmaker's shears for cutting out fabric, a pair of embroidery scissors or snippers for small tasks like cutting thread, and a pair devoted to paper to cut out patterns. (Don't even think about using your fabric scissors on paper—it will dull them in an instant. How is it that paper is stronger than steel?)

ASSORTED NEEDLES You'll want to find the perfect needle for the projects you do. Look on page 15 for a complete discussion.

THIMBLE To thimble or not to thimble, that is the question on page 15...and maybe the answer, too.

MEASURING TAPE & STRAIGHT EDGE When I'm in the throes of a project, I have been known to get very approximate and use anything handy for measuring. ("It's the length of my right index finger, minus one knuckle.") I've become a squinty master at eye-balling. However, a more precise and organized sewist might like to keep a tape measure and ruler/straightedge handy as it is pretty essential when first cutting out a project. I have a long stainless steel ruler that I use for marking straight lines. A measuring tape, either the standard cloth or vinyl tape or a cute little retractable one, should be tucked into your sewing kit to quickly take the guesswork out of sewing tasks. A really excellent tool for real life is to know your own hand width for on-the-fly measuring: With your hand wide open and flat on a surface, measure the distance from the tip of your thumb across to the end of your pinky. Mine is a practical eight inches, which comes in handy measuring everything from the length of a fabric remnant to the width of that adorable little side table at the antique store. Good news is it's always right there when you need it.

STRAIGHT PINS, SAFETY PINS, & PINCUSHIONS One of the many wonders of hand sewing is that without the need to send fabric under the speeding needle of a sewing machine, the whole process of pinning gets easier and less stressful. You no longer have to worry about breaking a pin in a little explosion of metal under the presser foot of the machine. Basting becomes completely unnecessary! Another hand-sewing timesaver! I prefer long, fine pins with big, colorful heads, but use whatever you like. I'm a sucker for vintage pincushions, and love to shop for them in junk stores and online auction sites. However, often my pins just end up in a little silver bowl on my work table. Use whatever makes you happy. You'll want safety pins in a couple different sizes for pulling elastic through casings. They can also be used in lieu of straight pins to secure a seam when you take a project on the road.

MARKING PEN There are lots of things on the market for marking your fabric. Disappearing ink fabric pens are my personal favorites. I like the ones that let you rub the ink with a damp cloth to make it disappear. Other pens have ink that fades after a short time, which I am never fast enough for and find myself marking and re-marking and rushing like a mad woman. Colored pencils are a close second for me, though I sometimes find I have to press too hard to get a good line. Tailor's chalk is another good alternative, though I find the chalk line too chubby for my taste. Keep an arsenal of two or three alternatives, since what marks well on a fine, solid-color cotton might be indistinguishable on a thick, richly-hued upholstery cloth.

EXTRA & OPTIONAL STUFF Some quilters swear by beeswax, but I find smoothing the thread with moistened fingers works just as well without having to cart around one more thing.

The great thing about hand-sewing is that its slower pace makes mistakes less likely. So you may never need a seam ripper at all. When I'm sewing with a machine, I am constantly ripping out seams made in the heat of the moment and regretted later. For this entire book of hand-sewing projects, I think I only had to remove one line of stitching.

When working with extra-thick fabric or a project with lots of layers, needle-nose pliers can come in handy. That little bit of extra leverage when pulling the needle through can be indispensable.

STANDARD
SEWING BASKET

SCISSORS

ASSORTED NEEDLES

MEASURING TAPE

STRAIGHT EDGE

PINS & PINCUSHION

MARKING PEN

THIMBLE

SAFETY PIN

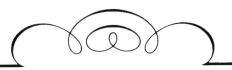

MATERIAL CONCERNS

The fabric stash is a capricious thing. We all have one filled with treasures, but so often, when we dive in,

we find that what-we-have is different from what-we-need. The fabrics that form the basis for the projects in

this book are varied, yes, but really fall into pretty tight categories. They are easy things to add to the stash,

so you'll always have some inspiration—of the material kind—right at your fingertips.

LINEN This fabric, in its natural color, is used in many projects (tote bag, pillows, etc.). I am a firm believer in having a couple yards of linen, in my favorite earthy colors, hanging around at all times. It is fabric that can be used for so many things and always lends a bit of sophistication to anything made from it.

COTTON CALICO An absolute must in any good stitcher's stash. The prints are cheerful and infinitely varied, in yummy colors that let you play joyfully like you used to with that great big box of crayons. Calicos are a great way to experiment with color theory and to learn the myriad ways that chroma charms the eye and penetrates the heart. Fat quarters of these charming, colorful prints cost pennies, so don't hesitate to play, play, play.

WOOL This is an almost magical fiber that can be transformed into a world of useful and beguiling fabrics. Rough yet soft, rugged yet refined, it is wool's dual nature that makes it so alive with possibility. Wool can also be one of the most pleasurable fabrics to work with. I like to give wool a hot-water wash and dry or two before I use it. This shrinks the fibers a bit, tightens up the fabric, and "felts" it a little. Be it a wool flannel or suiting, a wool knit or a recycled sweater, this treatment makes the fabric fluffier, softer, and the edges almost fray-free.

SPECIALTY FABRICS Gossamer sheers, silky lining fabrics, and retro linens might not all be front and center at the local fabric store. However, there are a wealth of possibilities if you venture off the beaten track. It is really worthwhile to snoop around on the Web for some of your fabrics, as they have specialty items—like 100 percent cotton sheer gauze or adorable linen prints imported from Japan—that just don't find their way into the big box stores. The Internet is also a great place for interesting notions and trims. Check the auction and craft sites; you'll be surprised at how many folks out there have tastes as unique as yours.

VENI, VEDI, VINTAGE I came, I saw, I had to have it! This seems to be a bit of a problem for me when it comes to vintage textiles, trims, and notions. There is something about the old stuff I find at flea markets, junk stores, auction sites, and in my grandmother's old sewing drawer that calls to me. Some of my favorite things are vintage linen kitchen calenders and old embroidered pillowcases, discarded men's dress shirts, and don't even get me started on old crumpled cotton lace.... But when swooning over old things to sew anew, you must be careful. Fibers are organic, and just like us they start to break down over time. Stick to non-structural uses for old things—for instance, don't sew something beautiful with old thread—and use your age wisely on things like buttons and trims.

THE EVOLUTION
of
THE NEEDLE

The first sewing needles were made from bone and wood and were used to sew animal hides. The oldest known needle is thought to be over 25,000 years old. Ancient Egyptians had needles of copper, silver, and bronze, and an iron needle dating back to the 3rd century was found in Germany. During the Middle Ages, bookbinders and shoemakers used hog bristles to make needles, while Native Americans fashioned theirs from porcupine quills. Muslims in Spain, seeking better tools for suturing wounds, perfected the metal needle in the 11th century and needles from the Arab world were prized in Europe through the 17th century when the needle maker's craft took hold in England.

Modern needles are made from high carbon steel wire, that is nickel- or gold-plated for corrosion resistance. The highest quality embroidery needles are plated with two-thirds platinum and one-third titanium alloy to keep them sharp and avoid breakage. "Gold-eye" needles are plated with gold to make them glide easily with less friction through fabrics.

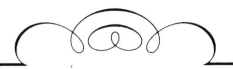

THE TRUTH ABOUT NEEDLES

Hand sewing needles have different names depending on their purpose. There are sailmaker's needles, chenille needles, tapestry needles, and doll needles, as well as at least a dozen more, each more specialized than the last. Needle size is denoted by a number on the packet. The length and thickness of a needle increases as the size number decreases. For example, a size 1 needle will be thicker and longer, while a size 10 will be shorter and finer. Easy enough, but this system breaks down when you get to embroidery or tapestry needles where the numbers jump to 14 and 18 even though the needles are fatter. To keep it simple, we will confine ourselves to the needles most suited to the home sewing and most practical for the projects in this book. I think you will only need a couple of packets of needles, a few fat and a few thin, to do all the projects in this book.

FOR GENERAL SEWING Get yourself a sweet little packet of assorted hand sewing needles or "sharps" that have a sharp point, a round eye, and are of medium length. There will be a nice variety of thicknesses and lengths. Each one probably has an ideal purpose, but the truth is that everyone has their own unique preference. Certain needles just feel right and good in our hands, they're just the right thickness, and just the right length. I have been known to bond so deeply with a specific needle that I will tear the house apart trying to find it rather than using one of the innumerable others in my sewing basket. I like a medium-fine needle that is on the long side. A longer eye is preferred as it makes for easy threading.

FOR EMBROIDERY OR TOPSTITCHING When you are working with heavier threads or embroidery floss, you'll need larger needles that can incorporate the thicker fiber. There are lots of different types that all sort of fall under this category. Some names to look for are: embroidery needles, crewel needles, darners, or Sashiko needles.

All these needles have sharp tips, and a larger eye to accommodate embroidery threads and thicker yarns. (Tapestry needles are not suitable to sewing fabric as they don't have a sharp point.) The crucial thing here is to get a needle that has a large enough eye to get your thread or yarn through, but not so large that it is difficult to pull through the fabric's weave. That's why a long eye is desirable to one that is wider; each has the same capacity for thicker threads and yarn, but the narrow, long eye fits through a tighter weave. The best way to explore the world of large-eye needles is to go into a store that carries them and look at the various types. I like to buy a packet or two and try them out. I can't stress enough how individual the needle preference really is. Needle manufacturers make all kinds of charts with correlations to thread type and fabric weave and technique used, but the truth is that until you hold that needle in your hand, thread it up, and send it dipping and diving though a scrap of fabric, you just can't know if it is the needle for you. Try lots of needles, find the ones you love, and guard them like treasure.

LONG THREAD, LAZY GIRL

"Langes Fädchen faules Mädchen." Now I am a girl who can be lazy with the best of them *and* I have always tried to avoid as much needle threading as possible. So this nagging old saying—oft repeated by my "just so" Swiss grandmother—always seemed written just for me. But these days, when hardly an hour goes by that I don't find a needle and thread in my hand, I have come to see the wisdom of this Teutonic truth. My newest mantra is re-thread your needle early and often! Just get over it! It is simply a constant in hand-sewing, and really, how long does it take? All those long threads that seemed so efficient: psshhh, false economy! Those long threads find a way to wrap around all the pins in your project, the nearby pincushion, around the scissors on the table next to you—even around the buttons of the shirt you are wearing. It is astounding really. It acts like a fishing line, catching and reeling in everything within a two-foot radius. It is mischievous, inventing trouble, and wasting more time than you ever save by changing it less often. I'm a convert to shorter threads—about the length from your hand to your elbow and then half as much again. I think I'll teach a new "old saying" to my granddaughter (if ever I might have one): "Long thread, cranky stitcher."

THREAD FOR THE MODERN WORLD

Hand sewing encourages you to let all your stitches show, and since stitches are made of thread, you'll want to choose it carefully. The projects in this book use lots of thicker threads, yarns, flosses, and ribbons, and the cursory discussion here will arm you with the information you need to navigate the tangle of possibilities out there.

FINE THREAD Most thread you see in the fabric store is **cotton-wrapped polyester,** the polyester core for strength and the outer wrap of long-staple cotton for smoothness and luster. It works on all fabrics, natural or synthetic, knit or woven, which is why it is called "all-purpose." It comes in a seemingly infinite array of colors. **100 percent cotton** thread is perfect for natural fiber projects that have no stretch to them. **Silk** thread has a beautiful sheen and is a dream to sew with–it is perfect for fine fabrics and delicate wovens, an obvious choice when hand sewing silk. Some stitchers swear by **quilter's** thread, which is often a fine cotton thread with an extra smooth finish that promises to make the thread resistant to tangling and easier to pull through multiple layers of fabric.

HEAVYWEIGHT THREADS Threads are sized so that the larger the number the finer the thread; so while an all-purpose sewing thread might be a 50 or a 35, a heavyweight thread might be an 18. **Toptstitching** thread is one step heavier than all-purpose, but not as hefty as my favorite thread for hand sewing called **button, carpet, and craft** thread. It is about the heaviest "true" thread designed for hand sewing where extra strength and durability are required. But I like it because it really shows off the stitches. It has a glacé finish to prevent tangling and abrasion. The typical fabric store variety is the time-tested combination of a polyester core wrapped in cotton. There is also a **100 percent linen** version that is becoming more widely available. The color palette on these heavy threads is limited, though their simple, natural colors are actually part of the charm.

FLOSS AND YARN Next up in the scale of prominent stitches are the embroidery flosses and yarns. There are two main types that are of interest to a hand sewist: embroidery floss and pearl (or crochet) cottons. The biggest and most visible difference between the two is this: The **embroidery floss** is a flat, untwisted collection of strands while the **pearl cottons** are made of two plies of fiber twisted together. The floss makes a slightly fluffier, more embroidered-looking stitch, while the pearl cotton simply looks more like a very thick thread. Each has its charm. Pearl cotton is available in several sizes, from the almost yarn-sized #5 to the thick-thread of #12. Size #12 is one of my favorite "threads" for topstitching. Both pearl cotton and embroidery floss come in cotton in a wide variety of colors, but nowadays embroidery floss in 100 percent linen is also available. It is truly gorgeous stuff, almost enough to inspire a hand-sewing project–with prominent topstitching of course–all by itself.

RIBBON A very simple stitch, when sewn with an interesting thread, quickly becomes a bit of art. Flat silk ribbon, the kind made for ribbon embroidery, brings a magical bit of elegance to anything it touches. Make sure you don't try to stitch with regular silk ribbon, as it is too thick to pull through most fabric. Look for ribbon embroidery silk through online retailers or where embroidery supplies are sold.

The SECRET LIFE of *Knots*

KNOTS ARE THE BEGINNING AND THE END OF ALL

your stitching, and as such deserve your devotion and respect.
Though I do love to see a knot well tied, often the most successful
knots are those that go unseen. They are the secret underground
foundation to all your carefully laid stitches. And, like all good foun-
dations, they dictate the success and longevity of that which is built
upon them. Here are the basics along with a couple of variations.

TYING ON { the single hand, tangled knot }

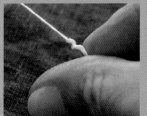

Wet your thumb and
index finger and grab the
thread near the end.

Wrap the thread twice
loosely around your
finger.

Slip the loops of thread
down off your finger.

Rub the loops back and
forth between your fin-
gers until the loops start
to spiral together.

Grab the thread just
above the twisted loops
and start running your
fingers down the thread.

Tighten the twisty
snarl into a knot.

TYING ON
{ the two-hand knot }

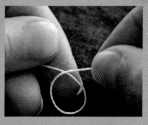

Make a loop in
the thread.

Send one end
through the
loop.

Wrap around
the back, and
send the end
through the
loop again.

Pull on both
ends of the
thread to
bring the knot
together

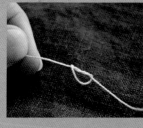

and tighten it
down.

Cut off the
thread leaving a
1/2-inch tail.

TYING OFF
{ and sinking the thread tail }

Make a loop in the thread and send your needle through the loop to make a knot.

Hold tension on the loop to bring the knot right to the end of the stitch.

Press your finger on the knot point and pull to tighten the knot.

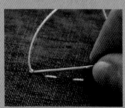

Sink your needle into the base of the knot and pull the thread through to the other side.

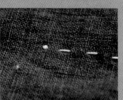

Here is your demure-yet-secure knot.

On the other side of the fabric, pull the thread taut and snip the thread as close to the fabric as possible.

The thread will spring back into the fabric and disappear.

HIDE YOUR KNOTS WHENEVER POSSIBLE. Looking for good places to tuck them away? Pull the starting knot up between two layers of fabric so it will be hidden in between the fabric. Place one under a seam allowance; on the underside of a hem you are starting (so the knot is on the underside of the hem edge); or on the inside of the gap before you close it with a slipstitch. When tying off, always send the tail of the knot deep into the nearest abyss, be it the inside of something stuffed, or along the underside/inside of a hem, etc. Let the needle come back up through the fabric a few inches away from the knot, pull it taut, then cut off the thread right at the base. The thread end will retreat into the fabric, and there will be no loose thread ends to mar your perfect stitches.

the *Running Stitch*

This is the simplest of stitches, the one that most people learn first. It is used—in a number of variations—for seams, topstitching, gathering, and basting. Each variation involves a slightly different rhythm or stitch length but each is based on the needle dipping in and out of the fabric at regular intervals. For a seam or topstitch, the length of the stitch and the distance between stitches should be even and between $1/8$ and $1/4$ inch. Gathering stitches are generally equal and wide; a $1/2$-inch stitch length works well. Basting stitches are often uneven, with the length of the stitch being about $1/8$ inch

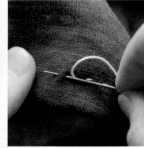

and the distance between being $1/2$ inch. The smaller stitch on top "locks" the thread, while the longer stitch on the bottom makes for a quicker seam. For topstitching, a short even stitch is typical. Neat, tidy, even bites make the topstitching look good... but not too perfect. Hand stitchers are not machines, nor would we want to be. Part of the charm of the handmade project is seeing the slight imperfections that highlight the character of the maker's hand.

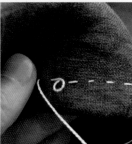

the *Backstitch*

The backstitch is the backbone of hand sewing. It is the strongest seaming stitch in the tool kit. Done well, it can almost seem like a machine stitched seam. The motion of the thread in this stitch is basically a loop-de-loop, with tiny backstitches locking tight the longer forward stitches. The technique is simple: The thread comes up through the fabric, makes a short stitch backwards, then down to the underside of the fabric where a long forward stitch is made, then up through the fabric again to make another small backstitch.

Half Backstitch
(side view)

This stitch is commonly used in two forms. What I call a "backstitch" (sometimes called a "continuous backstitch") looks and acts most like a machine stitch. It's formed by a short backward stitch on the top side of the fabric (about 1/8 inch), then a forward stitch that is twice as long (1/4 inch) on the underside of the fabric. The stitches on the topside almost touch, making a continuous line of stitching. The other one is called the "half backstitch." In it, the long forward stitch on the underside can be three to four times as long (say 3/8 to 1/2 inch) as the tiny (1/8 inch) backward stitch. The stitches on the top of the fabric do not touch one another but make a tidy line of perfect little stitches.

The half backstitch can work well on many seams, but the regular backstitch is necessary where a strong, long-lasting seam is needed and on slippery or fine fabrics like silk. This is also the best stitch for elastic casings.

The bottom line is that both versions of the stitch are very stable, so use whichever one you're most comfortable with.

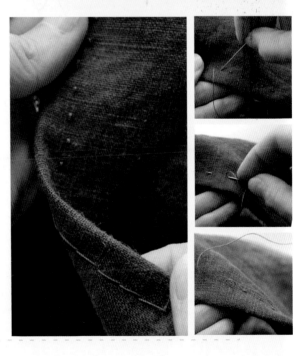

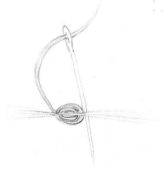

Stem Stitch

This is a simple embroidery stitch that can be used to good effect in regular sewing projects for outlining something or "drawing" a line on fabric with heavy thread or embroidery floss. It is almost like a backstitch, but worked so the long stitches are on the top of the fabric. Bring the thread up from the backside and make a stitch about ¼ inch long. Bring the needle back up about ⅛ inch from the initial insertion spot (about halfway); make another ¼-inch backstitch and repeat. For a cool effect when using thick floss, bring the needle up right through the strand of yarn.

Slipstitch

The key to this stitch is stealth...and tiny stitches. It is used to bring two folded edges together—to close a gap in a seam from the outside without anyone being the wiser for instance. Bring the thread up from the backside so it comes out at the top of the folded edge. Dip the needle tip into the folded edge directly across on the other side of the gap. Send the needle along inside this folded edge about ¼ inch. Let the needle tip cross back over to the folded edge on the other side of the gap, travel another ¼ inch or so, and bring the thread up through the top of the folded edge. All the forward motion of the thread is hidden inside the folds, and only the tiny stitches that cross the gap will show...but just barely.

Quilter's Tack Stitch

This is the stitch used by quilters to connect layers of fabric, batting, and backing together and to create a charming little pucker and accent stitch in the process. Bring the thread up through the fabric and stitch over ¼ inch or less, then down through the fabric, then back up at almost the same spot as before. Stitch up and down like this two or three times until you are happy with the stitch.

Blanket Stitch

This looks like a fancy stitch, though it is effortlessly easy to do. It is a perfect decorative edge for a blanket. To start the stitch, bring the needle and thread through the fabric from back to front about ¼ inch down from the top edge. Bring the thread straight up and over the top, then bring the needle through right at the base of the previous stitch. Bring the thread up to the top edge again, but this time go under the previous stitch so the thread is held in place at the top edge. Now send the needle through from front to back, ¼ inch down from the edge, and ¼ inch over from the last stitch. As the needle comes out the back, send it up and through the loop formed by the thread coming from the preceding stitch. Cinch it tight. Now the needle comes down to the front again, ¼ inch down, ¼ inch over, and once again goes through from front to back diving through the loop at the top edge.

Tack Stitch (on edges)

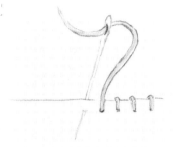

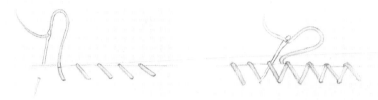

Overcast Stitch

This stitch for finishing raw edges can almost be considered the hand-stitcher's equivalent of the zigzags of machine stitching. You can either do this stitch straight up and down, as shown here, or slanted, as seen in step one of the Bi-color Overcast stitch at right. Bring the thread through from the back of the fabric about ¼ inch down from the fabric edge. Let the thread go up and over the fabric edge and then put the needle back through the fabric from back to front about ¼ inch over from the preceding stitch. Repeat, being careful to make consistent stitches. This stitch can also be used to connect an appliqué to a base fabric, using the same technique as described above.

Bi-color Overcast Stitch or Double Whip Stitch

This is a two-part stitch that can be worked in one or two colors. Start with an overcast stitch similar to the one at left, but keep the needle perpendicular to the edge so the stitches slant. Work all the way across your edge in this slanted overcast stitch with the first color. Then make a row of slanted stitches in the other direction in the second color. For this second row of stitching, the needle should come from the backside of the fabric and go under the stitch from the completed row right where it goes over the edge of the fabric. Take the needle down on the front of the fabric, and dip the tip of the needle through–from front to back–right at the base of the next stitch from the first row.

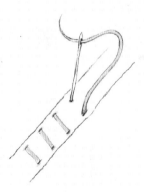

Diagonal Stitch

Appliqué Stitch

This is just a fun and novel way to attach a piece of plain trim or a ribbon to fabric. The diagonal threads give this stitch a fanciful look that belies its incredible simplicity. Bring the thread through from the back side, then make a short stitch at a 45° angle on your fabric and trim. Send the needle back through to the back. Bring the needle over horizontally, come through from the back side, and repeat the short stitch at a 45° angle. Repeat as needed to attach the ribbon or trim.

BIG SOFT SPHERES

for LITTLE TINY PEOPLE

Perfect for your budding superstar, these soft and squishy playthings are lovely to kick and roll and throw and catch and even just hug.

MATERIALS	**TOOLS**	**FABRICS**
scraps or fat quarters of light-weight cotton prints (each ball requires 6 different prints)	standard sewing basket { *see page 11* }	**FOR THE SPHERES:** Since this will be used by a child, organic fabrics would be an excellent choice here. You really only need a few inches of each print, so raid your stash for suitable scraps.
heavy-duty thread	paper for template	
fabric scraps for stuffing	washing machine/dryer	
eco-friendly fill (see note under Fabrics)	stiff brush (optional)	**FOR THE STUFFING:** This is a great project to try eco-friendly fillings like those made of organic cotton, kapok, and bamboo.
bell or rattle (optional)	Template page 122	

SIZE Spheres in two sizes, 6 inches or 8 inches in diameter

NOTES

Since these soft toys will be getting a lot of love and squeezing and maybe even a nibble or two, the stitching must be nice and tight to keep the stuffing safely on the inside. Use a small backstitch that has virtually no gaps to make it secure. For even more security, do a double row.

PORTABILITY FACTOR: { **pretty high** }
Small pieces, very few notions, sew them anywhere, but leave the stuffing for home.

Backstitch

1 Prewash all the fabric for this project—very important! Cut out six of the pattern templates on page 000 in the size you choose. The balls are most fun if each section of is a different fabric, so raid your deep stash! Try to position the template at a 45° angle to the grain of your fabric; this will give the best fray. Save all the cuttings and scraps (more on that later). { *photo 1* }

2 Wet each cut piece and rub it vigorously between the palms of your hands to rough up the edges as much as possible. Repeat the process until you see the edges start to fray. Once you have roughed up the edges on all the pieces, throw them in the dryer with something rough (like towels or jeans). This will help the edges really "bloom," creating the soft, fuzzy fray that makes these balls so lovable. Continue the entire fraying process until you are happy with the amount of fray. You can see why it was so important to pre-wash your pieces—otherwise they might all have shrunk to different sizes through all this wetting and drying. Lightly iron your sections so they lay flat, but not so much that you squash the fuzzy edge. { *see top left photo opposite* }

3 Lay out your sections in a pleasing sequence, alternating dark and light, tone or pattern until you are happy with the effect. Remember that the pieces at the far left and far right will ultimately be adjacent to one another when the sphere is complete.

4 Lay the first two sections on top of the other with wrong sides facing. Pin then sew along one edge from point to point about ¼ inch or less from the edge, using a backstitch and heavyweight thread. Start and stop about ¼ inch from each point to leave room for the point of the adjacent piece. Knot your thread at the end of the stitching, but no need to cut it as you can use this same thread when sewing on the next piece.

photo 1

photo 2

photo 3

5 Pin on the next piece to this first group, lining up the points, wrong sides together. Sew as before. Continue until you have attached all six pieces. Leave open the last seam for stuffing.

photo 4

6 To give the ball a little more heft than just plain stuffing can provide, bundle some of the fabric scraps and maybe a jingle ball in a small square of scrap cotton. Squeeze it together into a small ball, then tie off the top with a few stitches and a knotted thread. Wrap stuffing (I used bamboo fiber stuffing) around this bundle and stuff it inside your fabric sphere. Keep adding stuffing until the ball is round and firm. Make sure to work stuffing all around your bundle to keep it in the center of the ball. It is hard to over-stuff these spheres. { *photos 2 and 3* }

7 Pull the final two edges together and pin. You will need to compress the stuffing a bit to finish this seam, but it will spring back nicely. { *photo 4* } Sew the final seam closed. Knot and bury the thread deep inside the ball. If necessary, you can tidy up the apexes of your sphere, where all six points meet, and close it off completely with a few little stitches.

THREAD CADDY

<u>and</u> PIN HOLDER

As indispensable as it is charming,

this pincushion holds six spools of

thread at-the-ready while moonlighting

as a natty little piece of tabletop art.

MATERIALS	TOOLS	FABRICS
three 12-inch squares of wool or wool-blend felt, one each in sage green, cream, and heathered gray	standard sewing basket *{ see page 11 }*	**FOR THE FELT:** The best felt to use is 100 percent wool felt. It's thick and gorgeous and doesn't get pills or look ratty with age. A less pricey and easier-to-find option is a wool-and-rayon-blend felt. That's what I used here. Don't even bother with the synthetic felts. They look cheap and don't hold up to hard use.

a few small scaps of contrasting color felt to make the top knot

a circle template (even a bottle cap will work in a pinch)

heavy-duty thread in a couple different colors

> Template
> page *122*

approximately 12 inches of ¼-inch ribbon or cord

SIZE Makes one 8-inch caddy

NOTES

The caddy shown here holds six larger-sized spools of thread. If you use small-sized spools, you could probably get eight of those to fit around the same-sized caddy. See the option for an eight-compartment caddy in step 6 of the instructions that follow.

PORTABILITY FACTOR: { very high }
Small pieces, very few notions,
ready-to-use in no time.

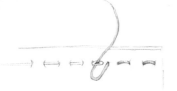

Running Stitch

**BEWARE the
SIREN CALL of OLD
THREAD**

I love shopping in junk
stores or sifting through
grandmother's sewing
basket for lovely old
notions, preposterous
buttons, and odd little
tools. There are inspiring
treasures to be found—
but old thread isn't one
of them. The fibers in
thread break down over
time. The weakness may
be unnoticeable while
you are working, but
then, suddenly, your
project may just fall to
pieces. And that is just
too sad to contemplate.

1 Cut two circles, each 8 inches in diameter, one from the cream and one from the green felt. Cut a smaller, 5-inch circle from the gray felt. You can use the templates on page 122.

2 Sew a line of running stitches around the perimeter of the two larger circles, about $1/8$-inch in from the edge. Use a heavy-duty thread in a color that stands out on the felt. { *photo 1* }

3 Stack the two large circles on top of each other, lining up the edges. Pin the smaller circle in the center. Stitch around the perimeter of the gray circle but leave a 2-inch section open.

4 Stuff the inner circle full of the batting to make a nice little mound in the middle. { *photo 2* } Once the stuffing is in place, finish stitching the circle closed.

5 Picture a clock in your head, then pin the two larger circles together at the 12, 2, 4, 6, 8, and 10 o'clock positions. Then sew a tack stitch about $1/2$-inch from the edge to secure the two circles together at each of these positions. If you want to store eight smaller spools in your caddy, imagine you were cutting a pizza to envision where your eight tack stitches should go.

photo 1

photo 2

6 Cut out eight approximately 1-inch felt circles of varying colors. Stack them one atop the other. Send a needle armed with heavy-duty thread up through the stack a little left of center. Stitch back down through the stack about ¼ inch away. Pull the thread until the circles fold in on themselves to make a pretty little bauble. Knot the thread securely, but don't cut the thread or remove the needle. (See the opposite page.)

7 With the threaded needle from step 6, find the center of the stuffed gray circle and sew the top knot into position. Sew through all the layers of circle three or four times to secure the top knot in place.

8 Thread the ribbon through the first spool of thread, then send it between the two larger circles of felt to the inside of the tack stitch. Thread it through the next spool of thread and again between the two layers and below the next tack stitch. Work your way around the caddy, adding spools until all the spaces are filled up. Pull the ribbon tight to bring up the sides of the caddy. Tie the ribbon into a secure bow knot and cut off any excess ribbon.

FINISHING TOUCHES

Make a top knot for the caddy that is both decoration and handle. It's a simple stack of felt circles—I cut these using a bottle cap for a template. It's easy to thread the spools into your caddy; the ribbon going through the spools acts as an axle for the spool to spin on so you can roll off just the length of thread you need. When a spool is empty or you need a different color, just thread on a new one!

BUTTON-DOWN APRON

made from RECYCLED SHIRTS

A little creative cutting and stitching allows you to "borrow" seams and buttonholes from a pair of recycled men's shirts to make a fetching and functional apron that gets down to business in the kitchen.

MATERIALS	TOOLS	FABRICS
2 large or extra-large men's long-sleeved, button-down shirts heavy-duty white thread	standard sewing basket { *see page 11* } iron (optional)	**FOR THE APRON:** light- to medium-weight cotton or linen button-down shirts, preferably with pockets and sewn plackets. Oxford stripes, small plaids, or chambray solids. Flannel shirts in stripes and plaids could make a handsome—and cozy—apron too. 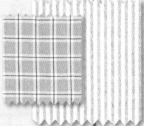

NOTES

Nice quality men's button-down shirts are a-dime-a-dozen at thrift stores and yard sales. Due to the relatively conservative color palette that is in favor, it's pretty easy to find two shirts that look natty together. To make an apron as nice and functional as this one, both shirts should have sewn-down front plackets. The shirt for the top bib of the apron should have a generous breast pocket—preferably with a button.

SIZE One size fits most

PORTABILITY FACTOR: { pretty high }
Fun and easy to sew anywhere.

SHIRT ONE: For the apron bib, neck strap, and waistband/ties

apron bib   neck strap   waistband/ties

The apron bib should be about 11 inches wide by 13 inches tall. The neck strap should start with the entire button side placket. The waistband pieces are 2½ inches wide by a minimum of 60 inches total length.

SHIRT TWO: For the apron skirt and pocket backing

apron skirt   pocket back

The apron skirt should be a minimum of 27 or 28 inches by 17 or 18 inches. The pocket back should be about 18 inches by 8 or 9 inches.

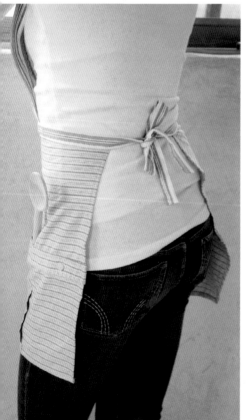

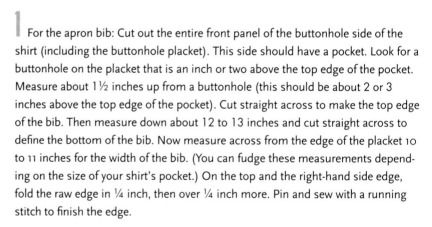

1 For the apron bib: Cut out the entire front panel of the buttonhole side of the shirt (including the buttonhole placket). This side should have a pocket. Look for a buttonhole on the placket that is an inch or two above the top edge of the pocket. Measure about 1½ inches up from a buttonhole (this should be about 2 or 3 inches above the top edge of the pocket). Cut straight across to make the top edge of the bib. Then measure down about 12 to 13 inches and cut straight across to define the bottom of the bib. Now measure across from the edge of the placket 10 to 11 inches for the width of the bib. (You can fudge these measurements depending on the size of your shirt's pocket.) On the top and the right-hand side edge, fold the raw edge in ¼ inch, then over ¼ inch more. Pin and sew with a running stitch to finish the edge.

2 To make the neck strap: Cut the button side placket from one shirt, cutting it close to the stitching on the finished edge. If you are using a loose weave fabric that threatens to fray a lot, cut the shirt front side of the placket with an extra ½ inch of fabric that can be folded over twice and sewn to finish the edge. (On a tighter weave, this will be unnecessary.) The bottom edge of the neck strap/button

photo 1

placket will already be hemmed. Attach the hemmed end to the top right corner of the apron bib (about an inch down from the top) with a double row of stitching across the top edge of the bib, catching the strap. { *photo 1* } I added a little cross of stitching just to make it doubly secure. The actual neck strap is formed when you button the other end to the buttonholes on the left-hand side of the apron bib. The many buttons available on the placket make the neck strap length fully adjustable.

photo 2

photo 3

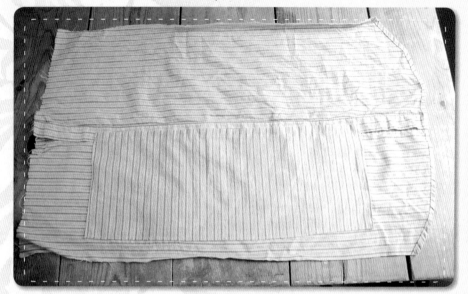

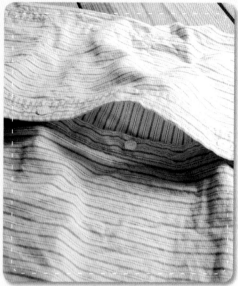

photo 4

3 For the apron skirt: The apron skirt is made from the entire front of the second shirt turned on its side, so the button front creates a large pocket that runs along the bottom edge of the apron. Cut out the front of the shirt, removing the collar and sleeves, and square off each side and the top of the shirt front. Leave the bottom hemmed edge as is. Fold the top edge of the shirt front down ¼ inch, then a ¼ inch again, and pin and sew to hem. Cut a rectangle of fabric from the back of the shirt or from the sleeve that is about 8 x 18 inches. This will be the back of the apron pocket. Fold all the perimeter edges back ¼ inch and press with an iron. Position the pocket back on the wrong side of the shirt front with its top edge running along the button placket of the shirt. { *photo 2* } Unbutton the placket on the shirt front and with a tight running stitch, sew the pocket back into place along the bottom edge of the button placket. Extend this stitching out to the ends to close the button placket on the shirt. Now stitch around the entire perimeter of the pocket back to form the large apron pocket. One large pocket is a little unwieldy for holding tools, so break up the expanse horizontally by buttoning every other button, then sewing a line of stitching down from each closed button to the bottom of the pocket. { *photo 3* }

4 To assemble the apron: From the back or sleeves of shirt 1, cut lengths of fabric about 2½ inches wide to make the waistband/ties. Seam these pieces together to make an overall length of at least 60 inches. (If you are using a shirt with a prominent stripe, try to match the stripes on the waistband so the seams won't be too obvious). Fold the ends back ½ inch, then fold the long edges in ½ inch, then fold in half lengthwise to make the waistband about ¾ inches wide. Press to crease. { *photo 4* }

Center the bib on the apron skirt with right sides together. Pin to hold. Center the waistband over the top edge of the apron skirt and the bib. { *figure 1* } Work down the length of the waistband/ties, pinning then sewing the folded edges together to make the ties and enclose the raw edges of the apron and bib. A running stitch, sewn about ⅛ inch in from the edge, works best here. Once the waistband/ties are attached, flip the apron bib up and sew a second row of stitching along the top edge of the waistband to hold the bib upright and finish the assembly of the apron. { *figure 2* } Now that you have whipped up this delicious little apron, time to whip up a little something for dinner!

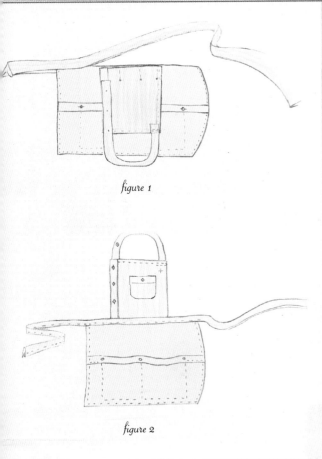

figure 1

figure 2

SHEER CURTAINS

with RIBBON STITCHING

Here's a practical, beautiful project where your hand stitching is both structural and decorative at the same time. Narrow silk ribbon becomes your "thread," transforming the lowliest of fabrics—loose-weave sheer muslin—into an elegant, airy, cloth confection.

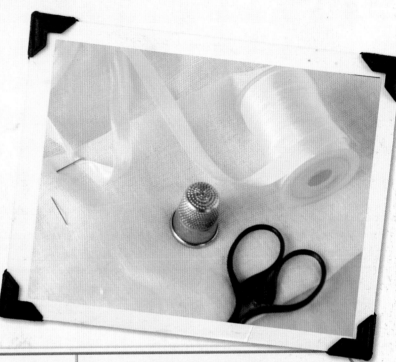

MATERIALS	TOOLS	FABRICS
2 or more yards of open weave, sheer white cotton at least 44 inches wide ¼-inch (10mm) soft silk ribbon See Notes below for yardage requirements.	standard sewing basket { *see page 11* } large embroidery needle	**FOR THE CURTAINS:** Choose an open-weave, sheer fabric like a cotton gauze, scrim, harem cloth, or voile. You want something that resembles a fine cheesecloth. **FOR THE RIBBON:** Make sure it is silk ribbon for ribbon embroidery, as this is a much lighter, finer, softer ribbon than the ribbon used for bows. There are lots of great sources online.

NOTES

Your window size will dictate the exact amount of yardage and ribbon needed. The width of the fabric will limit the height of the curtains, so if you have tall windows (more than 38 or so inches), these curtains will be cafe curtains that cover just the bottom half of the window.

To figure the amount of ribbon needed, multiply the width of the curtain times 7. Then add 2 times the height.

SIZE make a custom size for your windows

PORTABILITY FACTOR: { low }
Unless you have tiny, hobbit-sized windows, these will require a lot of fabric, making them unwieldy to take afield.

photo 1

photo 2

photo 3

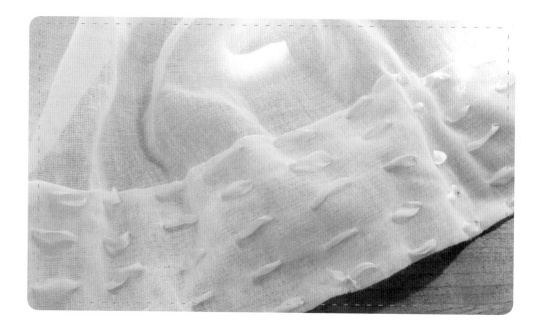

1 Measure each individual window and, based on those dimensions, cut fabric to the following size: Add 7 inches to the desired height of your curtains, and double the width of your window plus 2 extra inches for the side hems. For example, if you were making curtains to fit a window area that was 30 x 30 inches, you would cut fabric 37 x 62 inches.

2 For the hems along the sides of the curtains, turn the raw edges in ¼ inch, then turn under another ½ inch. Pin. Thread the embroidery needle with the narrow silk ribbon. (A length of about 3 to 4 feet is a comfortable length to start with.) Knot the end and begin working a running along the rolled hem about ⅜ inch in from the edge. When stitching with ribbon of this size, each stitch should be about 1 inch long. { *photo 1* } Repeat on the opposite edge of the curtain.

3 To make the bottom hem, fold up the raw edge ½ inch, then fold up another 3½ inches. Pin in place across the full width of the the curtain. { *photo 2* } Starting at the top edge of the folded hem, sew across with the ribbon using a wide running stitch. { *photo 3* } You can cut a piece of ribbon the width of your curtain plus 5 or so inches if you want to avoid any knots along the breadth of the hem. This will be a long piece and might be a little bit fiddly to work with. A knot or two within the hem is not really a problem. Just knot the new ribbon to the old and cut the ends short–about ½ inch long. At the end of the hem, knot the ribbon on the surface and sink the end inside the hem to hide. Repeat to sew across again, this time along the bottom edge of the hem. Match the stitch length and rhythm to the top row of stitching. Then add two more rows of stitching at even intervals between the top and bottom row. You can eyeball this or use a disappearing marker to draw a series of parallel lines on the hem to follow.

4 For the top curtain rod casing, turn down the top edge ½ inch, then again about 2½ inches. Pin and sew a row of ribbon stitching along the bottom and top edges of the casing to secure. Send your curtain rod through the casing and hang your new curtains.

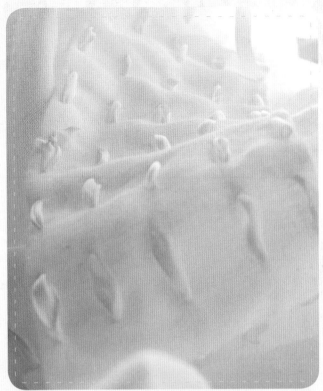

OWIE PUFFS

for BOO-BOOS

Life is full of hard knocks, but these adorable thermal packs are made to soothe. Sized to fit the biggest bumps right down to the smallest scuff, they are the perfect gift for kids—both young and old.

MATERIALS	TOOLS	FABRICS
small scraps of linen or cotton	standard sewing basket	**FOR THE FRONTS:** linen, medium-weight cotton in tiny, kid-friendly prints
contrasting pattern or colored linen, cotton or flannel for backing	{ *see page 11* }	
heavyweight thread or embroidery floss	straight-edge	**FOR THE BACKING:** linen, brushed cotton, flannel in stripes or solid
uncooked rice grains	spoon	
dried lavender or rosemary (optional)		

SIZE Makes three bags:
4¼ x 9 inches, 3¼ x 6¼ inches, 3 x 4¼ inches

NOTES

These little hot/cold packs can be thrown into the freezer for an hour or two to become a soothing alternative to the traditional hard, plastic-y ice pack. They can also be heated up in the microwave to loosen tight muscles or slowly warm chilly fingers in the winter.

PORTABILITY FACTOR: { pretty high }
Though the pieces are small and easy-to-sew on the go, filling the thermal pack with rice is best done at home

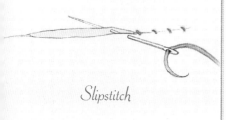

Slipstitch

OWIE PUFFS
for BOO-BOOS

1 To make the large pack, cut a piece of printed linen and a piece of backing fabric 4¾ x 9½ inches. For the medium, 3¾ x 6¾ inches, and for the small, 3½ x 5 inches.

2 With right sides together, sew a line of tight backstitches about ¼ inch from the edge around the perimeter. Leave a space open about 2 inches long, for turning and filling the pack. Clip the corners at a 45° angle. { *photo 1* }

3 Turn the pack right side out through the open seam. Poke (from the inside) or pick (from the outside) the corners to make a nice, crisp rectangle. Spoon uncooked rice grains into the pack. Mix in lavender if you wish to add a pleasant and soothing scent. Fill until the pack feels full and there are no empty areas, but be careful not to overfill. You want the pack to conform to the body part it is going to soothe. Once filled, pin the seam opening closed. { *photo 2* }

4 Use a slipstitch to close the opening. Repeat to make all three packs. { *photo 3* }

5 Use heavyweight or embroidery thread to sew a line of decorative topstitching around the perimeter of each bag. The stitching should be about ⅛ inch (or a tad more) away from the edge. This stitching will also reinforce the seam to keep any rice from escaping.

6 If you would like, add a center X stitch in the medium and large packs. These add a cute finish to the packs and also keep the rice from shifting too much and makes it a little firmer (another reason not to overfill the pack in step 3). Leave the smallest one without an X; it is the perfect size and density for a hot compress to soothe a tiny ear's ache.

photo 1

photo 2

photo 3

PERSONALIZED BIBS

with FRAYED EDGES

Nothing honors a new arrival on the planet more than a personalized gift sewn by hand. These bibs seam together the funky with the sophisticated, the soft with the rugged, to make an heirloom keepsake that is perfectly practical, too.

MATERIALS

¼ yard (or a fat quarter) of linen, plain or printed

¼ yard (or a fat quarter) each of solid cotton in four colors

colorfast fabric paint or ink (on inkpad) for the monogrammed bib

1 vintage kitchen calender towel, preferably linen, for the birthday bib

about 18 inches of ribbon

2 buttons (optional)

heavyweight or embroidery thread

TOOLS

standard sewing basket
{ *see page 11* }

tracing paper for pattern

washing machine/dryer

alphabet rubber stamps

stiff brush to hasten fray (optional)

> **Template**
> page *120*

FABRICS

FOR THE FRONT: medium-weight linen or linen/cotton blend in natural or in a fun, youthful print (see Notes)

FOR THE BACKING/PADDING: cotton solids in bold, saturated colors that look nice together

SIZE Each bib is approximately 8½ x 11 inches

NOTES

The retro calender kitchen towels were a mainstay of the 1960s kitchen and can be found at almost any junk store as well as all over the Internet auction sites. The adorable linen print comes from Japan, and can be found easily and inexpensively online and or at the more progressive fabric and quilt shops.

PORTABILITY FACTOR: { pretty high }
The stitching can be done anywhere, but you'll need to be near a washer/dryer for the final touches.

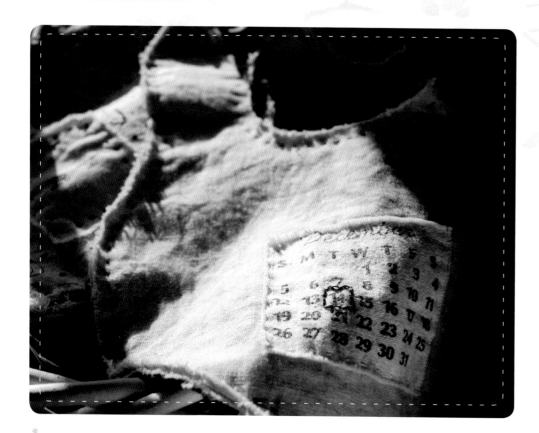

photo 1

photo 2

1 Using the template provided on page 120, cut one bib shape from the linen fabric and then one each from the three solid color cottons. Stack them one atop the other, lining up the edges. Make sure you put the color you want on the back of the bib at the bottom of the stack. { *photo 1* }

2 Using heavyweight thread, sew a line of running stitches around the perimeter of the stacked bib pieces about 3/8 inches in from the edge. { *photo 2* } To even the edges of the four layers of fabric, trim to about 1/4 inch away from the stitches.

3 Now is the time to send your bib through the washer and dryer to fray the edges. One good cycle should do it, but you might want to rough up the edges a bit after washing (and before drying) to make sure the edges really bloom. Once dry, if you want more fray, you can use a stiff brush to tatter the edges, or repeat the wash/dry process until the desired effect is achieved. Trim any loose threads.

4 Cut two pieces of sturdy ribbon about 9 inches long. Knot one end. Fold the other end over about 1/2 inch. Pin the folded edge (with fold side down) about 1/2 inch down from the top, and in the middle of the bib "straps." Use a few tack stitches to hold it in place. Position a button to cover the folded edge of the ribbon, and stitch the button in place being sure to go through all the layers of the fabric. Repeat on the opposite strap. { *see photo on opposite page* }

Note: If you prefer not to use buttons on the bib, simply use a series of tack stitches or stitch in an X to secure the ribbon.

TO MAKE THE BIRTHDAY BIB:

From a linen or cotton vintage calender kitchen towel, cut the birthday month panel. Be sure to leave about ¼ inch around the edge of the dates. Make the cuts square with the grain of the fabric so the edges will fray evenly. Sew the month in place on the front center of the bib with a simple running stitch, going through all layers of the bib. Next, use heavy-weight or embroidery thread to stitch a square or circle around the birth date. A stem stitch works great for this.

simple stem stitch

TO MAKE THE MONOGRAMMED BIB:

Tear out a piece of cotton fabric about 2½ inches square. Tearing ensures that you are creating a square on the straight of the fabric grain so that it will fray evenly. Tearing also creates a frayed edge on-the-spot without the need to wash and dry or rough up the edges in any way.

Practice with the fabric inks on a square of paper first to get the letters for the monogram just the way you want them. Stamp the fabric with the letters. Follow the manufacturer's directions to ensure that the fabric ink will stay put through the multitudes of launderings that are part of a bib's life. I used heat-set inks that required ironing on a high setting to allow the ink to fuse with the fabric's fibers. Once you have the monogram square just so, position it in the center of the bib, and stitch around the perimeter about ⅛ inch from the edge to secure. Bon appetit to all the little ones!

The POWER of the PERSONAL

One of the many reasons we make things with our own hands is to craft something that is completely and uniquely one's own—like nothing else in our cookie-cutter world. Personalizing a project with a name, initials, or a birthdate takes its uniqueness even further, making it a tribute to someone you love. It gives them tangible, daily proof that they are in your thoughts and near your heart.

BUTTONED-UP TOTE

with HANDMADE BUTTONS

This bag has a certain breezy elegance that comes from the classic palette, the gorgeous linen, and the one-of-a-kind graphic buttons. Even if you think you have enough tote bags, this one insists you need just one more.

MATERIALS	TOOLS	FABRICS
½ yard each of medium- to heavyweight linen at least 54 inches wide, in natural and chocolate brown	standard sewing basket { see page 11 }	**FOR THE TOTE:** medium- or heavyweight linen
4 yards of cord or thin rope—3/8-inch is perfect	fabric marker or pencil	**FOR THE BUTTONS:** cotton or linen fabric with fun little prints or something graphic like numerals or words, vintage kitchen calen-ders, feed sacks, etc.
4 one-inch dome button blanks	iron	
4 small two-holed buttons	pencil with eraser (optional)	
heavy-duty or embroidery thread in white	spool of thread	

NOTES

Linen used to be a prohibitively expensive fabric. But these days it is widely available in a broad palette of colors at a very comfortable price. Linen can't help but lend a certain dignity and grace to any project. Even if it costs a tiny bit more, its beauty and durability make it worth every penny.

SIZE tote (not including straps) 16 x 14 inches

PORTABILITY FACTOR: { moderate }
This is the perfect on-the-go project, both while you're making it and after you're done.

figure 1

figure 2

figure 3

figure 4

1 Cut a piece of natural linen 15 x 22 inches. Cut a piece of brown linen 21 x 32 inches. Fold the natural linen in half lengthwise with right sides together. Sew a backstitched seam along the side and the bottom, ½ inch in from the edge. Do the same on the brown linen.

2 Slide the taller brown linen bag inside the natural linen bag, making sure that the right sides are together. { *figure 1* } Align the top edges and sew the two pieces together with a backstitched seam. Leave about 3 inches of seam open. { *figure 2* } Turn the piece right-side out through this gap. Use a slipstitch to close the gap. The brown linen piece will form a 4-inch border along the top edge of the bag. Press the corners of the brown inner bag into the corners of the natural linen outer bag.

3 Crease the top edge, then use heavyweight thread or embroidery floss to topstitch along the edge of the bag about 1/8 inch from the edge. Make sure these stitches are even on both sides of the bag.

4 Fold the brown border down toward the outside of the bag at the seam where the brown and natural linen meet. Topstitch the new top edge of the bag. { *figure 3* }

5 To miter the corners and give the bag shape, turn it inside out. Pull the corner of the bag downward with the point centered. Measure about 2½ inches from the point and stitch straight across through all the layers of fabric. { *figure 4* } Turn the bag right side out again.

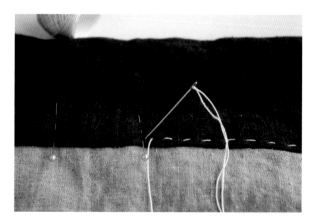

6 Sew the buttons into place on the tote bag. Each of the four buttons should be about 3½ inches in from the side of the bag, and centered top-to-bottom on the brown border. To keep the button secure, sew a smaller, two-hole button on the back side, going through the holes in the back button, then through the wire shank in the handmade button. Be sure to knot the thread around the shank several times before tying off to secure the button.

photo 1

photo 2

photo 3

7 Measure two pieces of cord or rope each 36 inches long. Make a circle out of each piece by overlapping the ends about ½ inch. Sew the two cord ends together with a heavyweight needle and thread, using several stitches in and out through them to secure. Make a long skinny loop of the cord, placing the seam in the middle of one long side.

8 To make the strap cover: Measure a piece of natural linen fabric about 3½ inches wide by 14 inches long. Fold both ends and both sides down ¾ inch and press. Center the cord on the strap cover and fold the edges of the fabric around the cord and overlap them. { *photo 1* } Sew through all the layers of fabric down the center channel between the two cords to make the strap cover. { *photo 2* }

9 Loop the strap ends around each of the two buttons on the same side of the bag. Make sure that the seam in the strap cover will face down when the strap sits on your shoulder and that the strap cover is at the center of the strap. Sew the two pieces of cord together tight to the base of the button with a few stitches. { *photo 3* } This will keep the cord from slipping off the button. Repeat on all four buttons.

MAKE YOUR OWN BUTTONS:

Find a scrap of fabric that has an interesting image or graphic on it.

Cut a circle of fabric about ¼ to ⅜ inch larger than the top of the button blank.

Fold the edges of the fabric circle over the spike-y edge of the button blank. Make sure the fabric catches on the edges. A pencil eraser works great to press the fabric down onto the little spikes.

Place the button back over the wire loop on the button blank. Line up the wire loop shank with the hole in a spool of thread push the button back down and snap it into place.

WOOL THROW

with APPLIQUÉD BORDER

This one's ridiculously easy and yet creates a
dramatic, sumptuous, one-of-a-kind throw.
You can customize the palette to match your
décor. It's the perfect winter project, keeping
you warm and cozy while you're working
on it and after you're finished.

MATERIALS

2 yards felted wool at least
54 inches wide

about ⅛ to ¼ yard felted wool in
5 or 6 different colors (I used sage green,
ivory, brown, and brick red)

embroidery thread or fine wool yarn
to match your blanket fabric

heavy-duty white thread for the appliqué

TOOLS

standard sewing basket
{ *see page 11* }

large sewing needle or
small embroidery needle

tracing paper for pattern

> Template
> page 121

FABRICS

FOR THE BLANKET: double-sided
wool flannel, mohair coating,
coat-weight cashmere

FOR THE APPLIQUÉS: Use felted
wools including wool flannel, boiled
wool, or 100 percent wool felt.
Be sure to choose wools that do
not fray when cut.

NOTES

The size of this blanket is dictated only by the width of the wool.
Many good quality coat-weight wools come in 60-inch widths, which
make an ample throw—even wide enough for two to snuggle beneath.
For the length, 2 yards (about 6 feet) is nice. For most folks,
that is enough to keep both your toes and shoulders covered
while relaxing in your favorite chair.

SIZE 54 – 60 inches x 72 inches

PORTABILITY FACTOR: { low }
...but perfect for stitching on a
cold winter's day by the fire or in front of
a Jane Austen movie.

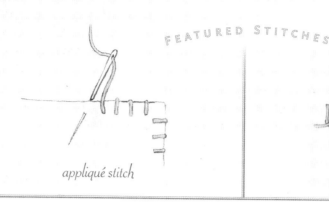

FEATURED STITCHES

appliqué stitch

blanket stitch

1 Trim and square up the edges of your wool piece. { _photo 1_ } Mark a line with marker about 10 inches from the bottom edge as a guide for your border.

2 Cut out the colored wool for your border using tracing paper and the template on page 121. Lay out the pattern of rectangles and circles at even intervals across your blanket and adjust to fit. To make the design more jaunty, some of the rectangles should sit high on the line, others low, and others in the middle. Pin into place. { _photo 2_ }

3 Cut out 1-inch strips of white wool for the borderline. Cut them long enough to fit between the rectangles plus about ½ inch. Tuck the ends ¼ inch under the rectangles on either side and pin into place.

4 Using a medium needle and heavy-duty white thread, begin working to attach the first section of white strip using the appliqué

stitch. Then stitch around the first rectangle along both the outer and inner edges. (Be sure the white strip on the opposite side is tucked under before you stitch the rectangle.) Knot off.

5 To apply the circle of felt in the center of the rectangle or as the flower element on the blanket variation, start by bringing the thread up through the center of the circle from the back. Sink the needle down at the edge of the circle and come back up at the center. Now sink the needle down at the opposite edge of the circle and come back up at the center. Work around the circle until it is cut up into eight sections (as you would cut a pizza). Finish with a double knot at the center. { _photo 3_ }

6 Appliqué the rest of the border rectangles and strips across the blanket.

7 Finish the perimeter of the blanket using a blanket stitch worked in embroidery thread or light-weight wool yarn. { _photo 4_ }

| _photo 1_ | _photo 2_ | _photo 3_ | _photo 4_ |

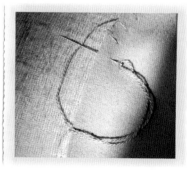

VARIATION

Once you get the hang of this simple form of appliqué, infinite embellishment possibilities await you. Here is an alternate blanket with a border inspired by simple botanical shapes.

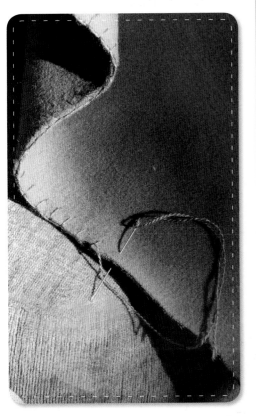

PILOT HAT

from RECYCLED SWEATERS

One can never wear too many hats. This little capper might look complex, but is easy to sew from felted and fluffy recycled sweaters. Handmade, frayed trim tape makes it both a little sweeter and a little more edgy at the same time.

MATERIALS

5 different-colored recycled sweaters or sweater scraps

about ½ yard 100 percent cotton print fabric to compliment the sweater palette

sewing thread

embroidery thread in a bright complementary color

TOOLS

standard sewing basket
{ *see page 11* }

ruler or straight edge

tracing paper for pattern

washer and dryer

large needle for embroidery

Template
page *120*

FABRICS

FOR THE SWEATERS: Be sure to choose sweaters that are 100 percent wool so they will shrink and felt. "Superwash" wool has been treated so it will not shrink, so avoid anything with that label. Other natural fibers like cashmere, angora, or alpaca also felt beautifully.

SIZE One size fits most

NOTES

The palette should be yummy—try using colors that are closely related on the color wheel like pink, peach, and yellow. Extend those possibilities with light and dark versions of each color like shell pink to hot pink or pale peach to bright orange.

PORTABILITY FACTOR: { **pretty high** }
Once all the materials are washed and dried and cut and frayed, the hat pieces can be worked anywhere.

FEATURED STITCHES

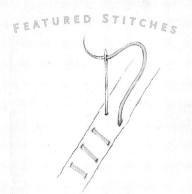

diagonal stitch

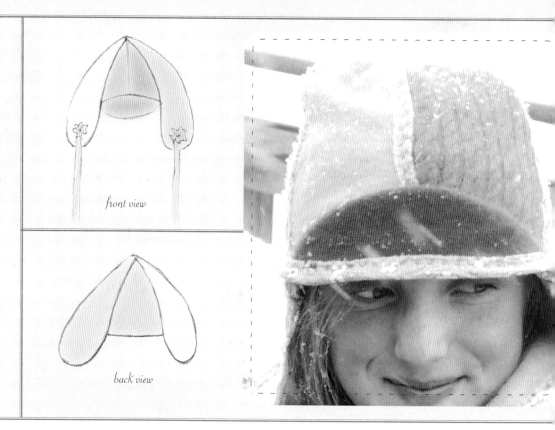

front view

back view

TO MAKE THE BIAS TAPE & TRIM:

Lay the cotton fabric out flat. Fold the bottom right hand corner up to meet the top edge of the fabric. Line the top edges up and you will have a fold diagonal to the grain of the fabric that is called the bias. Crease along this fold, open the fabric up, and cut along the crease, cutting away the right triangle. Measure, mark, and cut strips off the diagonal edge; cut six 1-inch wide strips and four ½-inch wide strips. Wet the strips, one at a time, under running water. Take a strip and rub it hard between the palm of your hands to roughen up and fray the edges. Keep re-wetting and rubbing until you can see significant fraying along both edges. Repeat with all the strips. Dry the wet strips in the dryer to finish the fraying and ruffling process. Remove from the dryer and press very lightly with a cool iron so the trim lies flat.

photo 1

1 Wash and dry all the sweaters to shrink the fibers together and turn the fabric into a felted, fray-free material. Some sweaters may require multiple washings to really tighten them up.

2 Use the template on page 120 to cut pieces out of the sweater fabric. To cut down on the number of sweaters needed, use the same color for the visor and the back.

3 With right sides together, start at the topmost point of each piece. Pin the pieces together starting with the back, sewing its right hand edge to the earflap piece, then the earflap to the first front piece, then to the second front piece, then to the opposite earflap that attaches to the back piece. Use a backstitch to make ¼-inch seams.

4 Turn the hat right side out. Start at the bottom edge where the two front pieces meet. Pin the narrower bias trim over the seam up to the crown of the hat where all the pieces come together. Cut off the bias trim at the top. Next, work from the bottom where the back piece meets the earflap and pin the bias trim over the seam, working up over the crown of the hat and down the other side to where the opposite earflap meets the front piece. Repeat this to cover the remaining seams. { *photo 1* }

5 Thread the larger needle with embroidery thread and use the decorative diagonal stitch to attach the bias trim to the hat. { *photo 2* }

6 Find the slightly rounder edge of the hat visor, and fold the wider bias tape in half over the fabric edge. Pin in place. Use the embroidery thread and a simple topstitch to attach the fold-over bias tape to the visor. { *photo 3* }

7 Next pin the raw edge of the visor to the bottom edge of the front of the hat with right sides facing. Be sure to match the center of the visor with the center seam of the hat front.

8 Starting at the back where it meets the earflap, fold the wider bias tape over the raw edge of the bottom of the hat. Work around the raw edge of the hat, being sure that the bias tape is centered around the edge. Pin in place.

9 When you come to the visor, fold the bias tape over the edge of the hat and the visor edge, where you've pinned them together in the step 8. This way, the bias tape both attaches the visor to the hat and covers the raw edge at the same time. When you come to the end of one piece of bias tape simply overlap the next piece on top of it an inch or so. No need to fold back or seam the splice as all the edges are happily frayed as it is. Work all the way around the bottom edge of the hat.

10 Use the embroidery thread and a topstitch to secure the bias fold tape to the hat.

11 To make the ties on the earflaps: Use the same technique to make the fabric flower as shown for the slippers on page 171, but use one of the frayed bias strips and leave it flat and unfolded to start. Use a gathering stitch along one edge to ruffle the strip into a spiral. Make a tighter spiral for this flower as you don't need a hole in the middle for this project. Take another piece of wide bias tape about 12 inches long, fold it in half, and sew it together with a running stitch. Attach the tie to the flower and attach the flower to the earflap about 1½ inches up from the bottom edge of the hat. Repeat to make the flower and strap for the other side.

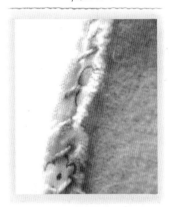

photo 2

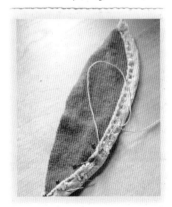

photo 3

photo 4

SWEET SLIPPERS

with SIMPLE PIPING

Making slippers feels like a substantial project. You feel connected to an ancient craft while cobbling away on these, yet no special skills or guild memberships are required. Actually, they are barely an afternoon's toil.

MATERIALS	TOOLS	FABRICS
1 yard of fleece or boiled wool	standard sewing basket *{ see page 11 }*	**FOR THE SLIPPERS:** fleece, boiled wool, cotton double-knit
¼ yard of cotton print (a fat quarter should be enough)	safety pin	
optional material for the sole	tracing paper for pattern	**FOR THE TRIM:** cotton calicos
quilt batting to pad the sole (a 12-inch square should be enough; if you want extra-cushy slippers, double it)		**FOR THE SOLE:** leather sole, rubber dots sole (both are available at fabric stores), leather, micro-suede, anything that doesn't fray
1 yard fold-over elastic in a color to complement your cotton print	**Template** page *123*	
sewing thread to match the fleece and the cotton print		

SIZE Fits women's sizes S: 6-7, M: 8-9, L: 10-11

NOTES

These slippers have a bit of give, so the sizing is flexible. If you live where the winters are arctic and plan to wear them with thick socks, choose the next size up.

PORTABILITY FACTOR: **{ high }**
Small pieces, few tools, impresses on-lookers

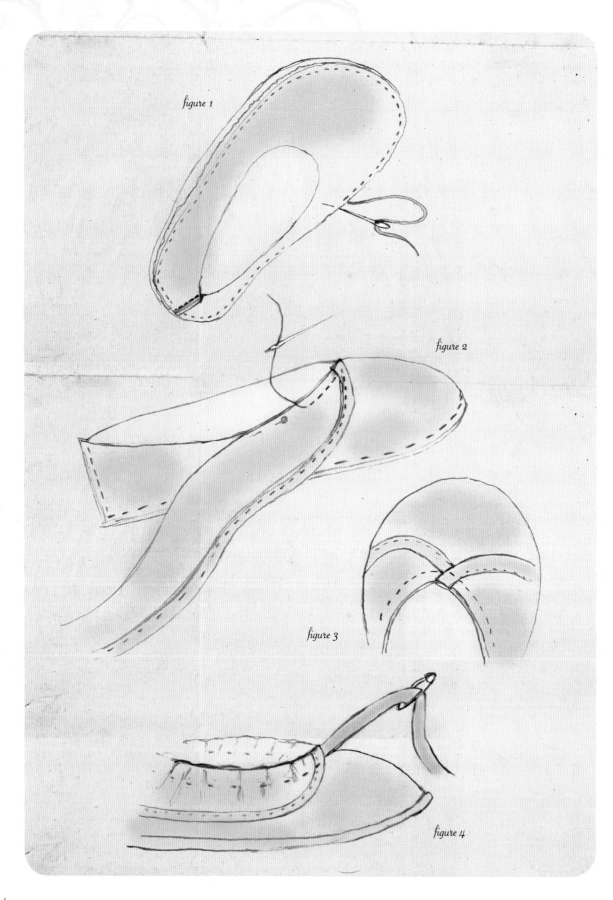

figure 1

figure 2

figure 3

figure 4

1 To make the seam binding: Cut a piece of cotton print fabric 2 x 30 inches. Lay the cotton fabric strip flat on the table. Working from one end on the long edge, fold the edge in to the center of the strip of fabric and crease by running your finger firmly down the folded edge. Now fold the other edge into the center and crease that side. You won't be able to do this down the entire length of the strip all at once, but you can work in short sections. Now fold the strip in half down the center and crease. If you have an iron handy, iron the trim to flatten. If you are hard at work over a cup of tea at the cafe, improvise by grasping your folded tape firmly in both hands and rubbing it up and down on the edge of the table. { *photo 1* }

2 Using the template on page 123, cut the soles, vamp, and collar out of the fleece fabric. These can be cut out on the straight of the grain. Use the sole template to cut the batting and the optional sole reinforcement fabric. Trim about ½ inch off around the perimeter of the batting and reinforcement.

3 If using sole reinforcement material, stitch it on the outside of the fleece sole bottom. The fleece sole will extend beyond it all the way around. Sandwich the batting between the top and bottom fleece sole pieces. Baste to hold.

4 Fold the vamp piece in half with right sides together and stitch ¼ inch in from the edge to make the center back seam.

5 Find the center back of the heel on the sole and, with wrong sides together, line it up with the center back seam on the vamp piece. Find the center of the toe of the sole and the vamp, and line those up as well. Pin to hold. Work around the perimeter of the sole easing the vamp into place and pinning to hold. This is where your slipper will quickly take shape, going from flat two-dimensional pieces into three-dimensional shoes! Use a tight backstitch to seam the pieces together about ¼ inch in from the edge. Trim the seam back to about ⅛ inch. { *figure 1* }

6 With the right sides out, start at the center back of the slipper. Pin the trim on to cover the seam that connects the sole to the vamp. { *photo 2* } Work all the way around the perimeter of the sole concealing all the layers of the seam. Overlap the trim ends about ½ inch at the back and then fold the end of the trim under to create a finished edge. Use a tight running stitch to sew the trim into place. You'll definitely need your thimble to get through all the layers.

7 Make another piece of trim (see step 1), but this time start with a piece of fabric 1¼ x 24 inches to make a narrower trim binding. Apply the folded trim to the outside edge of the collar piece. Topstitch into place.

8 Turn the slipper inside out. Position the collar piece into place at the top edge of the vamp. At the center front, the two ends of the collar should overlap slightly. Pin then sew the collar to the vamp with a backstitched ¼-inch seam. { *figures 2 and 3* }

9 Turn the slipper right side out. Fold the collar pieces over the vamp seam to the outside. To make the casing for the elastic, sew a row of topstitching ½ inch down from the edge. { *figure 4* }

photo 1   photo 2

photo 4

10 Cut a piece of colored elastic about 12 inches long. Attach a safety pin to one end and thread the safety pin through the elastic casing at the top of the slipper. { *photo 3* } Once the elastic is all the way through, pull on the ends to even them up.

11 Thread the two elastic ends through the hole in the center of your handmade flower from page 71. Pull the elastic through so the top of the slipper is a little gathered, push the flower down to the base of the elastic, and tie the elastic ends together into a double knot. Cut off the ends of the elastic leaving about 1 inch. Use a tack stitch to secure the flower to the elastic knot and to the slipper. { *photo 4* }

12 Now repeat all steps for the other slipper!

photo 4

TO MAKE THE FLOWER:

Cut a piece of cotton fabric 2½ x 9 inches. Fold the long edges in ¼ inch toward the wrong side. Repeat on the other edge. Then fold the strip in half. Use a loose basting stitch to stitch the strip together and to serve as your gathering stitch. Be sure to knot one end securely while leaving the other end of the thread loose. Grab the loose end firmly and pull to begin gathering the fabric strip into a spiral. Gather until the fabric strip comes full circle and makes a flower. Seam the two ends of the strip together toward the back of the flower. There should be a little hole in the center of the flower just big enough to slip the tip of your pinkie through (you'll need this hole to attach your flower).

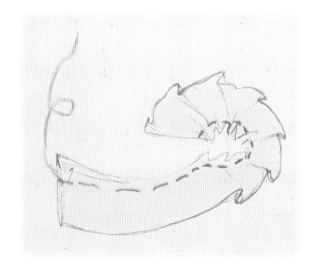

PILLOWS TIMES THREE

THREE VARIATIONS

Good design—like great music—requires finding a theme, then improvising variations upon it.

These three pillows reflect that creative principle, setting natural textures and earthy colors against the bold, intricate, one-of-a-kind embellishments.

MATERIALS

²/₃ yard of natural linen at least 54 inches wide for each pillow

small amounts of linen in the secondary colors:
¼ yard black for reverse appliqué pillow, plus scraps of other colors for the design
¼ yard brown for swirly pillow
1/₈ yard each of 4 or 5 colors for the ruffled pillow

3 or 4 yards of soutache or "middy" braid for swirly pillow

heavy-duty or embroidery thread in black and white

18 x 18-inch pillow insert for each pillow

TOOLS

standard sewing basket
{ see page 11 }

fabric marker or pencil

iron

Template
page *125*

FABRICS

FOR THE PILLOW: natural linen works beautifully for both the front and back of the pillow.

FOR THE EMBELLISHMENTS: linen or a linen/cotton blend for the embellishments and their backgrounds.

SIZE Each pillow measures 20 x 20 inches

NOTES

These pillows have an earthy palette with an ethnic, essential feel to it that plays beautifully off the natural, undyed linen background. Feel free to experiment with a different palette that works for your décor.

PORTABILITY FACTOR: { moderate }
You need a bit of table space for this one.

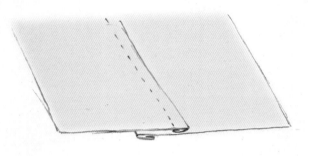

figure 1

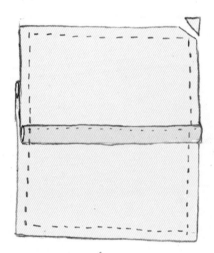

figure 2

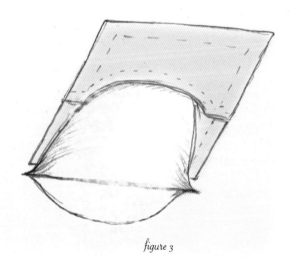

figure 3

TO MAKE THE BASIC PILLOW COVER:

1 For the pillow front, cut one piece of natural linen 22 inches square. (Try the technique described on page 77 to use the fabric grain as a cutting guide.) See the instructions that follow for additional fabric and techniques needed to complete the embellishment variations for the pillow front.

2 For the pillow back, cut two pieces of natural linen 22 x 15 inches. Fold the long edge (22-inch edge) of each back piece down first $1/4$ inch, then ¾ inches. Pin. Sew a line of tight top stitching to finish the edge.

3 Lay the pillow back pieces one on top of the other with the right sides facing up as shown in figure 1. Overlap the finished edges of the backs about 3 inches so that the whole piece forms a 22-inch square. Pin these two pieces together.

4 Lay the pillow front on top of the back piece with right sides facing. Match up edges and corners. (This is a little bit of a chore on the ruffled pillow because of the volume of the ruffles, but lay the ruffles down flat along the edge and pin securely). Pin around the perimeter, then use a backstitch to sew a seam about ½ inch in from the edge. Reinforce the area where the two back panels overlap by backstitching this section a second time. This will ensure that the seam doesn't fail when you put in the pillow insert.

5 Clip the corners at a 45° angle. { *figure 2* } Turn the pillow cover right-side out through the gap on the back side. Poke or pick the corners so they are sharp and square.

6 To create the soft border on the pillow cover, pin along the perimeter of the pillow cover. Sew a long, running stitch (peaks and valleys of the stitch should be ¼ to ½ inch each and should be 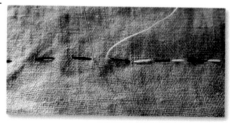 even) about 1¼ in from the edge, using heavyweight white thread. Next come back along the same seamline with black heavyweight thread, alternating stitches with the white as shown above (the white valleys will be the black peaks, and visa versa). Stuff the cover with the pillow insert. { *figure 3* }

TO MAKE THE LOOPS & SWIRLS:

1 Cut a piece of brown linen 7 x 22 inches. Fold over the long edges ¼ inch and pin or do a basting stitch to secure. Find the center of your pillow front and position the brown section of fabric so it's centered top-to-bottom and side-to-side on the pillow front. Pin in place.

2 Do a small, even topstitch with a heavyweight or doubled thread to sew the brown panel to the front along both edges.

3 Now the fun begins. Starting at one side of the pillow front, lay the soutache or flat ribbon on the panel in curves, swoops, or twirls. Don't try to pin the entire pattern on all at once. Do one curve at a time, pin it, then sew it on with the same thread and stitch from step 2. Part of the fun is making it up as you go along.

4 Work your way, swooping and swirling, and just generally squiggling all the way across the brown panel.

5 Follow the instructions on page 74 to turn the pillow front into a pillow.

GOING with the GRAIN

Sometimes it is a bother to find a big flat surface, and gather all the supplies to measure, mark, and cut one square or rectangle from your fabric. But there is an easier way:

Use the grain of the fabric as your cutting guide. Any woven fabric has a warp (vertical threads) and weft (horizontal threads). Grab one of these threads in either direction and start pulling on it. As the thread pulls out of the fabric, it leaves a one-thread wide empty space which is a perfect cutting line. Use this technique for all the pieces for your pillows. It's fast and perfectly accurate.

pull!

cut!

TO MAKE THE RUFFLED PILLOW:

1 Cut five strips of colored linen fabric 2½ inches by about 50 inches long. Be sure to cut the fabric strips along the straight of the grain so they will fray nicely. (See the note on the previous page about cutting on the grain.) Choose any color combination you want for the ruffles. I used one each of the terracotta, sage green, and brown, then used two of the neutral gray.

2 Pull a few threads from both of the long edges of the fabric strips to give it a nice frayed edge. Fold the strip in half lengthwise, and finger-crease the fold. { *photo 1* }

3 Sew a loose gathering stitch along the edge of the fold about ⅛ inch in from the edge. Pull the thread to gather the strip until it is the approximate length of your pillow front. Knot loosely, but leave the thread long in case the strip needs to be a little longer as you are sewing it on. { *photo 2* }

4 Mark the center of your pillow front top-to-bottom and draw a straight line edge-to-edge with a fabric marker or pencil. Open up your folded fabric strip and center it along the line on your pillow front, starting at one edge. Put in a couple of pins to secure just the beginning, as it's best to pin a little and sew a little as you go along.

5 This part of the project would be dastardly to sew on a machine, so you are lucky to be using a needle and thread. You don't have to struggle to keep the machine from catching up the wrong piece of fabric, sewing down a ruffle, or running wildly into a thicket of pins. Just pin a couple of inches, then sew the strip in place, then pin a couple more until you have worked all the way across. A tight running stitch does the trick here. Put your needle right down into the valley of the fabric strip making sure to catch all the ruffles. Don't worry if the stitches are neat or what it looks like on the other side—no one will ever know! (Especially if you use a thread color that matches your ruffle.) { *photo 3* }

6 Repeat with the rest of the ruffles. Each subsequent ruffle should be placed fairly close to the one next to it. I found ½ to 1 inch worked nicely on my pillow.

photo 1

photo 2

photo 3

TO MAKE THE REVERSE APPLIQUÉ:

1 Cut a piece of brown linen 7 x 22 inches.

2 Mark the pattern on your fabric using a light-colored fabric pencil and the template on page 125. Or simply look at the template for ideas, then create your own design.

3 Now make the cuts in the black fabric. You don't cut *out* any fabric, you are simply making a slice in the fabric, and making little clips at angles, so you can fold back the edges to expose another color fabric behind. Best not to make all the cuts at once, or the fabric gets a little squirrely. Work the sections one at a time across the panel. { *photo 1* }

4 Cut a piece of colored fabric that is bigger than the design, and place it on the back side of the black fabric, covering the cuts from step 3. Pin to keep it in place. Turn back over to the front of your panel and carefully begin to fold and tuck the raw edges under along the cut. These tucks should be a little less than ¼ inch or so. Pin as you go. The angled clips at the end of your cuts allow you to make nice squared-off corners. { *photo 2* }

5 Use heavyweight or doubled thread to stitch down the edges about ⅛ inch in from the folded edge. Make sure your stitches go through all the layers of fabric. Continue adding cuts and colored backing fabrics until you have worked your way across the entire panel.

6 When the panel is completed, fold over the long edges ¼ inch and pin or do a basting stitch to secure. Center the panel side-to-side and top-to-bottom on the pillow front. Pin in place. Then use a small, even topstitch to sew the panel to the pillow front with a heavyweight or doubled thread.

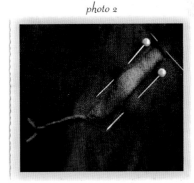

photo 1

photo 2

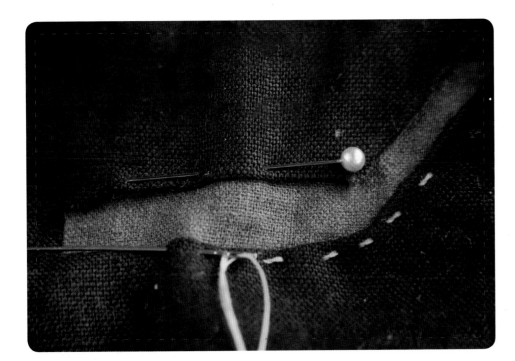

SEWING KIT

for ON-THE-MOVE STITCHERS

This clever little kit carries all the tools-of-the-stitching-trade. Even better, the very making of it teaches you all the stitches a competent hand seamstress will ever need. It's a tiny treasure that holds your gadgets, your notions, and a good bit of your stitch wisdom, too.

MATERIALS

½ yard of felt in charcoal gray

¼ yard of felt in green

scraps of cotton prints and felt for the cover design

embroidery floss in blue and green

heavyweight thread

¼ yard of thin black elastic cord

a few inches of ⅛-inch black elastic

small hook, two buttons, small wad of stuffing

TOOLS

standard sewing basket
{ *see page 11* }

straight-edge

embroidery needle

Template
page *126*

FABRICS

FOR THE FELT: Choose 100 percent wool or wool-blend felt because it will hold up better under heavy use. The polyester or acrylic felts pill, are static-y, and have a tendency to "catch" so things don't slide in and out smoothly. The wool/rayon blend felts are available even at the big-box fabric stores.

SIZE about 5 x 7 inches closed, 11 x 13 inches open

NOTES

Here is the perfect project to make your very own. The cover design can be done as shown, or you can use the simple techniques to create your own inspired design. Okay, so maybe it crosses the line from sewing to embroidery, but who cares? It is beautiful and deceptviely easy to do.

PORTABILITY FACTOR: { **pretty high** }
Once the pieces are cut out, it's perfect to work anywhere.

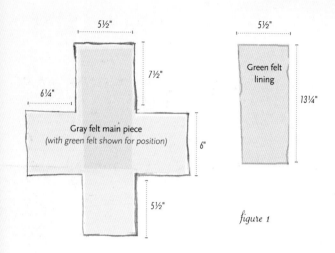

5½"
7½"
6¼"
Gray felt main piece
(with green felt shown for position)
6"
5½"

5½"
Green felt lining
13¼"

figure 1

photo 1

photo 2

1 Cut gray and green felt for the kit as shown above. Stack the pieces as shown and pin in place. { *figure 1* }

2 Fold up the bottom flap to make the larger inner pocket. Sew along the sides to secure, using heavyweight thread and a running stitch. { *photo 1* }

3 Fold the left-hand flap in half and sew around the right and bottom edges. Stuff with batting, then sew the top closed to make the pincushion. { *photo 2* }

4 Using your small sewing scissors as a guide, cut out a triangle of felt that is about ¼ inch bigger than the scissor blades all around to make a scissor pocket. Place a small piece of cardboard in the large center pocket of your kit to keep you from sewing the pocket closed while you stitch it into place. Use a simple overcast stitch to attach the triangle. Sew down both sides and sew about ¼ to ½ inch on the top edge to hold the scissors firmly. { *photo 3* } Now cut a tall skinny rectangle about 1½ inches wide x 4½ inches tall to create a place for markers or a tape measure. Position it next to the scissors pocket. Use the cardboard piece as before, but this time a simple running stitch works to attach the pocket.

5 Fold the right-hand flap in half and pin. Topstitch down the folded edge and leave the needle and thread attached for now. Cut the top edge at an angle starting about ½ inch lower than the folded edge, as can be seen in the photo opposite. For the tiny notions pocket, cut a 2½-inch square of gray felt. Cut a 1½ inch-wide slit in it, about ¾ inch from its top edge. Using a blanket stitch, sew around the perimeter of the slit. { *photo 4* } Sew this square into place at the bottom edge of the folded flap, being sure to sew it to the frontside of the flap only and not go all the way through to the backside. Topstitch around the perimeter. Now topstitch around the sides and bottom edge of the entire right-hand flap to make the flap pocket, this time sewing through all the layers. At the angled top, sew a topstitch through the outer pocket to finish it but not to close it. This pocket will hold a packet of needles.

6 Cut a piece of grey felt 3½ x 6 inches. Roll it up like a cigar and check to see that your thimble fits snugly on the end. If necessary, trim the roll until it fits the thimble. It should be tight. Sew the seam in the roll to secure. { *photo 5* } Sew a one-inch piece of black elastic on the green felt as shown in the photo opposite. Use little X stitches on either end to secure. { *photo 6* }

7 Sew buttons on the right- and left-hand flaps to close them when the sewing kit is packed up and on the move. Center them top-to-bottom and sew them on the edge of the flaps adjacent to one another. It doesn't matter if the buttons match—in fact it's more charming if they don't. Tie a thin piece of elastic cord around the base of one button, then tie the two free ends together to make a loop that will go over the other button to close the flaps. { *photos 7 and 8* }

8 Use the instructions and illustrations on the following pages to embellish the exterior flap and finish the edges with a decorative stitch. Once that is completed, finish the kit by adding a way to close it. Center and attach a loop of elastic cord on the bottom edge of the back of the sewing kit. Make a double knot in the cord and sew back and forth over the knot to attach the loop to the kit. { *photo 9* } Trim the ends of the elastic cord to finish. On the front cover, center and attach a store-bought hook or a button if you'd prefer. The loop of elastic should fit over it with just a little stretch to keep the cover snugly shut. { *photo 10* }

photo 3

photo 4

photo 5

photo 6

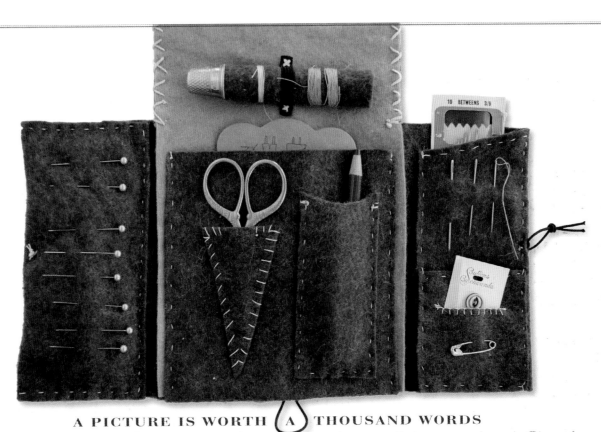

A PICTURE IS WORTH A THOUSAND WORDS

When in doubt about the instructions or if you just want to see where something goes, this picture tells the story most eloquently. Please refer to it as you are sewing to make the whys and wherefores perfectly clear!

photo 7

photo 8

photo 9

photo 10

bi-color overcast stitch

stem stitch

overcast stitch

blanket stitch

TO EMBELLISH THE COVER:

Choose the dragonfly template on page 126 or play with your own design using these simple techniques. Cut out narrow leaf or wing shapes and slip a piece of calico cotton behind it. Make sure the edges of the cotton overhang the cut edges of the felt by at least ¼ inch all around. Pin to hold in place, then topstitch around the perimeter to secure the fabric. Use an alternate color to add detail if you'd like. To make a simple flower or the dragonfly eyes, cut a circle of felt. Start at the center, bring the needle up from behind, and sew one stitch out to the bottom edge of the circle. Then bring the needle back up in the center, and stitch out to the right-hand edge of the circle. Work around the circle until you have split it into quadrants, then into eighths. Make a big obvious knot in the center. For the flower, you can add little stitches near the center in each of the sections you have just stitched. Use a running stitch to add details like the dragonfly's antennae or to sew on body parts. To create the two-toned stitching on the dragonfly's body, sew a simple running stitch in white, then come back with a running stitch with black thread that alternates in the spaces. Use a stem stitch to add detail like stems and tendrils to your stitched illustration. When you are happy with the cover, secure the gray cover to the lining of green felt using a simple alternating running stitch shown on the floral cover, or the beautiful bi-color overcast stitch that finishes the dragonfly cover.

CAFÉ NAPKINS

with BUILT-IN NAPKIN RINGS

These petite napkins are just perfect for

catching your morning croissant crumbs or

keeping you civilized over a light lunch.

They cleverly "borrow" the buttons and

buttonholes from a recycled shirt to make

napkin rings that are built in.

MATERIALS

bits and pieces of four men's
extra-large long-sleeve,
button-down shirts

thread to match

TOOLS

standard sewing basket
{ *see page 11* }

iron (optional)

FABRICS

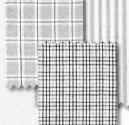

FOR THE NAPKINS: Use cotton,
linen, or hemp men's
button-down shirts with sewn
plackets in colors and patterns
that mix and match well together.
Long sleeve shirts offer two
extra napkins each.

NOTES

*There is a lot of engineering, clever stitching, and lovely fabric that
goes into a button-down shirt. These napkins offer a way to upcycle
those resources after a shirt has passed its prime. The placket offers
buttons and buttonholes that make useful built-in napkin rings.
They also offer a tidy way to hang the napkins when not in use.
Consider using this same design—but on a larger scale—to make
lovely, natural-fiber kitchen towels.*

SIZE Each napkin measures 12 x 12 inches

PORTABILITY FACTOR: { high }
Once the pieces are cut out,
work them anywhere.

photo 1   *photo 2*   *photo 3*

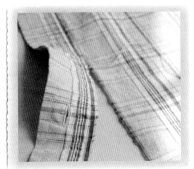

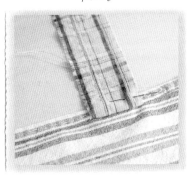

1. Cut squares of fabric from the back and sleeves of the shirts. I was able to cut able to cut two 13- or 14-inch squares out of the back and one out of each sleeve. But if you're like me, you'll want to cut just a couple out of each shirt so you can have a fun pastiche of different mix and match napkins.

2. Cut the button placket off of another shirt. Cut along the straight of the grain close to the folded edge. On a tightly woven shirt, you can cut close to the folded edge and leave it raw. If it's a looser weave that might fray, cut about 1/8 inch from the fold, then tease a couple of threads off to create a little fray. As long as it is on the straight of the grain, the fray will be stable and look great. { *photo 1* }

3. For the tab, cut the placket so that there is about 1 inch of length below a buttonhole, and about 4 to 5 inches above the buttonhole. Hem the short end (closest to the buttonhole) by folding it up 1/4 inch, then 1/4 inch again. Stitch to hem.

4. Now move onto the napkins. Hem the perimeter of the napkin by rolling the edge under 1/4 inch once, then 1/4 inch again. Pin to hold. If you like, iron the folded edges to hold them in place while you sew. Stitch a tight and even running stitch around the perimeter of the napkin. Stop stitching at the half-way point on the last side, but leave your needle threaded. Now is the time to mark the position for the tab.

5. To mark the tab position, fold the napkin in half along the napkin edge you left partially open. Mark the center. Then measure between the center and the edge, and mark the center of that area. Your tab will center on that mark.

6. Tuck the unhemmed end of the tab under the rolled edge of the napkin at the marked point with wrong sides facing. Pin. Test the length of the tab by rolling up the napkin and wrapping the tab around it. The buttonhole on the tab should be tangent to the edge napkin hem without rolling it too loose or too tight. If the tab is a bit long, cut some length off the end that is currently tucked into the napkin hem. Use the needle and thread from step 4 to finish the napkin hem, sewing the tab into place as you stitch. { *photo 2* }

7. Turn the tab up and stitch across it along the napkin hem about 1/8 inch from the edge. { *photo 3* } Now remove a button from the shirt placket and sew it onto the right side of the napkin. Position it on the hem and centered on the tab. This napkin is ready to roll!

PRETTY POTHOLDERS

with VINTAGE SMOCKING

Smocking is an old-as-the-hills sewing technique that is quite mysterious and magical. These potholders are a fun way to learn the basics and put all that sculptural padding and tufting to good use.

MATERIALS

¼ yard of linen or cotton for the front

¼ yard of medium- to heavyweight cotton for the backing

¼ yard of quilt batting

optional: ¼ yard of heat-resistant fabric

thread to match backing fabric

heavy-duty or embroidery thread

1 button

1 colored ponytail elastic

TOOLS

standard sewing basket
{ *see page 11* }

large needle for embroidery

iron

ruler

fabric marker

FABRICS

FOR SMOCKED FRONT:
Light- to medium-weight linens are my favorites for this, but even humble cotton broadcloth or muslin will work.

FOR THE BACKING: Any medium to heavyweight cotton is good in either a kitchen-friendly print or a solid.

SIZE Approximately 8½ inches square

NOTES

Smocking is a wondrous construction indeed. You might find yourself slightly obsessed with the incredibly interesting, fabulously springy, infinitely entertaining honeycomb/accordian piece of material you and your needle have created. This is what seamstresses used for elastic before elastic was created!

PORTABILITY FACTOR: { pretty high }
When you're doing the smocking, take it anywhere—you'll look like an expert seamstress.

Tack Stitch

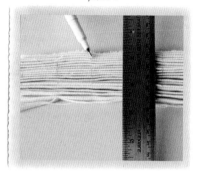

figure 1

1   Cut a piece of the fabric for the front 8½ x 24 inches. Using a water-soluble fabric marking pen, mark down ½ inch from the short (8½ inch) edge. Draw a rule across the fabric to mark your first foldline.

2   Move your operation to an ironing surface. Fold the fabric down along the marked line and iron the fold flat. Now flip the fabric over, and fold down ½ inch in the opposite direction, using your previous fold as a measurement guide for the next fold.   { *figure 1* }   Iron this fold flat.

3   You might remember doing something similar to this with construction paper in elementary school to make paper fans: Continue flipping, folding, and ironing your fabric down the full 24-inch length. Be sure to keep the sides as square as possible by making your folds straight. You will now have a rather tall, teetering stack of folds that are just a few inches wide.

photo 1

4 Keeping the stack of fabric tightly folded, measure in from the side edge ½ inch and mark across the surface of the folds. Then measure over 1¼ inches and mark across again. Do four more marks 1¼ inches apart and that should leave ½ inch remaining to the other edge. Make sure that the pen has touched the crest of all the folds as these marks will tell you where to stitch in the next step. { *photo 1* }

5 Thread a medium needle and bring the needle up through the first mark in the first pleat of fabric. Bring the second pleat over to meet it, and sew the two together with two or three tack stitches. End with the thread to the back side and send the needle down inside the crest of the pleat to the next mark on the second pleat. Come up through the mark and bring the third pleat over to touch the second one. Sew these two together with tack stitches. { *photo 2* } End with the thread underneath, and send the needle down the second pleat again, to the next mark. Come up through the fabric, bring the first pleat to meet the second one, and sew the two together with tack stitches. Continue zigzagging down the length of the pleats, alternating between stitching the first and second pleats together, and then the second and third. { *photo 3* } This approach means you will not need to knot off and start anew at every stitch point. The first row is by far the hardest, just getting the hang of the rhythm. Stay focused and stitch carefully until the emerging pattern makes everything more obvious. Once you've done a row or two, you'll have it mastered and the rest will be a cinch. When you reach the end of a row, knot off and start a new thread for the next row of pleats.

photo 2

photo 3

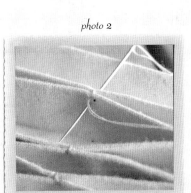
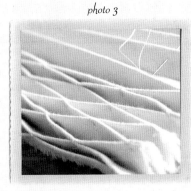

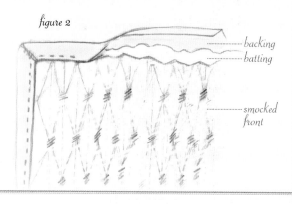

figure 2

backing
batting

smocked
front

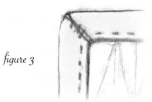

figure 3

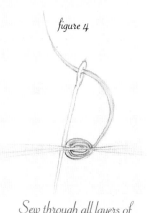

figure 4

Sew through all layers of fabric and batting right over the smocking stitches to quilt the potholder together.

6 Lay the smocked fabric face down on an ironing surface. Stretch it open slightly and press lightly with a hot, steamy iron. You don't want to obviously press it flat, you just want to square it up and make it stay open. Pull it open and stretch it on the diagonal, then do quick, glancing passes with the iron. If you flatten it too much, just turn it back over and re-crease some of the folds with your fingers. This should quickly bring back the dimension.

7 Cut out a square of cotton backing fabric that is about 2 inches wider and taller than the smocked piece. Then cut two pieces of batting that are roughly the same size as the smocked front. If you are using the heat-resistant fabric, cut it the same size as well.

8 Stack up the fabrics: backing fabric face down, then center the heat-resistant fabric (if using) face down on top of that. Next comes the two layers of batting, and lastly, center the smocked fabric face up on the stack. There should be an even margin of backing fabric around the perimeter. Pin in a few places to keep the stack secure.

9 Fold the raw edge of the backing fabric in about ½ inch all the way around and press. Begin working your way from the center of one of the sides, folding in the folded edge of the backing fabric over the "stack" to cover and enclose the raw edges. Pin in place. { *figure 2* } Once you have worked your way to a corner, fold the corner of the backing fabric at a 45° angle before folding it up and over the edge of the stack. This will make a nice, tidy turn in the corner.

10 Sew around the edging with a tight running stitch. A few extra stitches at the corner will bring the two angled folds together and close the gap. { *figure 3* }

11 To quilt the potholder together, use your embroidery thread and larger needle to go over the spots where the earlier smocked stitches are. Use a bright color so they really show. Be sure to go all the way through to catch all the layers. { *figure 4* }

12 I chose a hair elastic to make the hanging loop because I like a loop that is stretchy enough to fit over the odd-sized knobs and hooks in my kitchen. The hair elastics come in a zillion colors and work perfectly. Use a sharp needle and a double thread and sew the hair elastic together less than ½ inch in to make a smaller loop on one end. Send the needle straight through both sides of the elastic, then wrap the thread around the elastic several times, then send the needle through one more time and knot off. Sew the button on your potholder in the corner, about ¾ inch from the edge. Slide the small loop of the elastic over the button. It should be a tight fit, but you can add a few tack stitches to make it more secure.

photo 4

TREASURE BAG

with ZIPPER ROSES

These rich and precious bags can accompany you out for a night on the town, carry your valuables on vacation, or tuck into your top drawer to keep safe your most beloved keepsakes.

MATERIALS	TOOLS	FABRICS
¹⁄₃ yard of wool fabric for exterior	standard sewing basket *{ see page 11 }*	**FOR THE BAG:** Try men's wool suiting fabrics like tweeds, houndstooth, flannels. Also great in thick boiled wool or dense boucle.
¹⁄₃ yard of satin for lining		
one 9-inch metal zipper for the bag	craft scissors (to cut zippers)	
2 or 3 metal zippers for the roses, at least 18 inches long	iron	**FOR THE LINING:** Use a silk satin with lots of sheen in a jaw-dropping color and you will grin every time you open this bag.
2 or 3 metal buttons		
thread to match exterior and lining fabrics		
heavy-duty thread to match zippers		

SIZE Makes one 9 x 6-inch bag

NOTES

You can find vintage metal zippers in junk stores and on online auction sites, or raid your grandmother's sewing stash. Also, some modern zippers have metal teeth. Look for jacket zippers, replacement zippers for sleeping bags, or specialty zippers made for upholstery.

PORTABILITY FACTOR: { pretty high }
Small pieces and parts, easy to work anywhere.

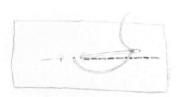

Backstitch

figure 1

figure 2

TREASURE BAG
with ZIPPER ROSES

1 Cut a rectangle of the wool suiting fabric 10 x 12 inches, and a piece of the lining fabric 9¾ x 11¾ inches. Fold the suiting fabric in half, right sides together, to make a rectangle 10 x 6 inches. Fold the lining the same way. Pin.

2 Starting at the bottom fold, use a double thread to backstitch a seam ½ inch in from the edge. Stitch to within ½ inch of the top edge, and turn and sew toward the center about ½ inch. Repeat on the other side, leaving an opening in the center for the zipper. Clip the corners at a 45° angle.

3 Fold down the edges of the top zipper opening ½ inch and iron flat. Repeat all these steps on the lining.

4 Turn the bag right side out. Position the zipper along the top edge of the opening of the wool outer bag. The metal stops at the top and the bottom ends of the zipper should be at the ends of the opening in the bag. Position the zipper on the inside of the bag opening so the zipper tape is on the inside of the bag and the folded edge of the fabric just meets the bottom edge of the zipper's metal teeth. Pin in place, working down one side of the zipper. At this point, it will help to unzip the zipper before working your way up the other side. { *photo 1* }

5 Ready your needle with heavy-duty thread. Beginning at the end of the zipper tape, work a half-backstitch or a backstitch down the length of the zipper. Sew about ¹/₈ inch in from the fabric edge. Be sure to add some anchoring stitches at each end of the zipper to reinforce. { *figures 1 and 2* } Now is the time to position your zipper roses and sew them onto the outer bag.

6 With the lining wrong side out, push it inside the zippered opening in the outer bag. Ease it down into position, pushing all four corners into place and making the top opening even with the opening in the outer bag. Check to be sure the right side of the lining is showing on the interior of the bag. { *photo 2* } Position the top folded edge of the lining on the inside of the zipper tape so it covers the stitching from the last step. Make sure the lining isn't touching the zipper teeth or it will tangle in the zipper. Pin in place. Use sewing thread that matches your lining to sew the lining into place. A tight running stitch that just goes through the lining and catches the zipper tape and the inside folded edge of the bag will do the trick and will not show on the outside of the bag. { *photo 3* }

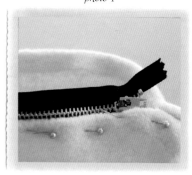

photo 1

photo 2

photo 3

UPPER LEFT: For the seams on the lining, backstitch with double thread.

UPPER RIGHT: Use a tight backstitch with a heavy-duty thread to sew in the zipper.

BOTTOM: Choose metal buttons with some interesting texture or intricate design.

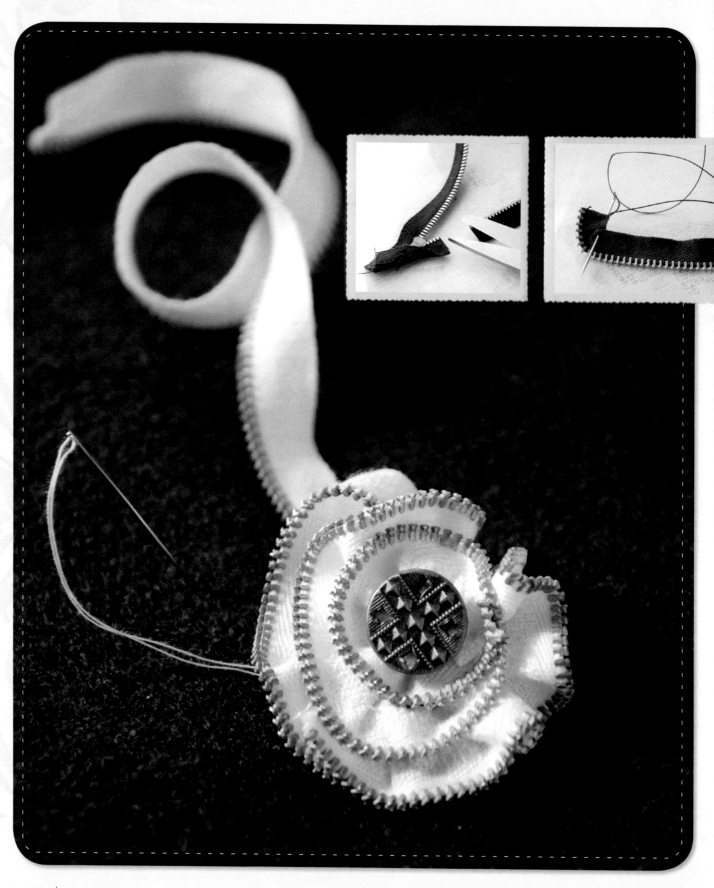

TO MAKE THE ZIPPER ROSE:

Cut off a long section of metal zipper, being sure to place the blades of your scissors between the metal teeth before you make the snip. (Don't use your best sewing scissors for this!) Thread the needle with heavy-duty thread. Begin at one end and start spiraling the zipper around the center. Fold little pleats in the zipper tape to make a circle and stitch through the pleats to secure the shape. After the first round, spiral the next circle around the back of its outside edge, still folding and pleating, and sewing the second round onto the first. Continue working around until you have three or four rounds. Use lots of stitches to keep the rose secure. Check often to make sure that your circles aren't too tight or loose, and that the rose is ruffly but can still lie fairly flat. When the rose is the size you desire, cut the zipper off and tuck the end of the zipper down and to the back of the rose. Secure with a stitch and knot. Bring the thread to the center of the rose and sew a fancy metal button into place. Voila!

SQUASHY HASSOCK

with FAT PIPING

Call it an ottoman, a footstool, or a hassock, this little gem is rich in character and texture. It is simple to make, yet can "make" a room. It is a useful piece of furniture that you can sew yourself, with nothing but a needle and thread.

MATERIALS

1½ total yards of heavyweight upholstery fabric or one 18-inch square for top
two 18 x 13-inch rectangles each for sides A and B
two 18 x 13-inch rectangles for the bottom

6 yards of ½-inch diameter fluffy cotton piping (sometimes called "filler cord") or a ½ yard of cotton batting

sewing thread plus embroidery floss for topstitching

four 1-lb bags of fiberfill or one large bag of polystyrene pellets and one bag of polyfill

optional: repurposed pillowcase to house stuffing

TOOLS

standard sewing basket
{ see page 11 }

optional: needle-nose pliers if needle is difficult to pull through

FABRICS

FOR THE HASSOCK: mid- to heavyweight upholstery or home décor fabric like chenille, tapestry, velvet, damask, linen, suede, corduroy, or crewel. Consider using scraps and remnants and mixing the patterns on the hassock's sides for a lush, old-world look. The patterns and colors can be individual, but the fabric weights should be consistent.

SIZE Makes one hassock 17 x 17 x 12 inches

NOTES

This hassock owes lots of its charm to the oversized piping that punctuates its perimeter, lending an overstuffed opulence to this humble little piece. You can either buy the oversized piping at your local fabric store, or you can cut strips of cotton batting a couple inches wide, then fold and stuff those along the edge seams. Once sewn into place, the batting gives the same beguiling effect.

PORTABILITY FACTOR: { moderate }
A bit bulky, this one, but I actually *did* sew mine at my son's little league game!

Half Backstitch

Running Stitch

SQUASHY HASSOCK
with FAT PIPING

1 Cut the following rectangles out of your fabric:

one 18-inch square for top

two 18 x 13-inch rectangles for A sides

two 18 x 13-inch rectangles for B sides

two 18 x 13-inch rectangles for the bottom

2 With right sides together, pin the four rectangles for the sides along each of the four sides of the hassock's top. Start stitching about ½ inch from the end of each side. Use a half backstitch, about ½ inch in from the edge, to sew them into place. { *photo 1* } Repeat around all four sides.

3 Bring two edge pieces together to form the corner of the hassock. Pin and sew ½ inch from the edge, again stopping the seam ½ inch from the end of the side. Repeat on all four corners.

4 To make the bottom, turn under one long (18-inch) side of the bottom piece ½ inch, then fold under another inch. Pin. Sew across to finish this edge. Repeat on the other bottom piece.

5 With right sides together, pin one bottom piece to the open end of the hassock, matching raw edges. Sew into place with a ½-inch seam. Be sure to add a few extra stitches to reinforce the beginning and end point of this seam, as it will have some added pressure on it later.

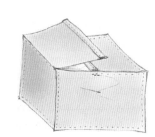

figure 1

6 Position and pin the other bottom piece along the remaining unfinished edges of the hassock bottom. { *figure 1* } The two finished edges of the hassock bottom will overlap each other to make an opening in the bottom of the hassock for adding the stuffing. Sew the second bottom piece in place. At the point where the two finished hems cross on the hassock bottom, you will be sewing through several layers of fabric. Here is where those optional needle-nose pliers may help pull a stubborn needle through the layers of fabric! You have now completed your cube. Turn the hassock right side out.

photo 1

photo 2

photo 3

7 Now it's time to add the fat piping: You will work first on the four side seams, then pipe the top perimeter edge of the hassock, then the bottom. Beginning at the bottom of one the side seams, press either the cotton piping or the strip of cotton batting right up against the seam. Work your way up the seam, pressing the cotton stuffing firmly in place and pinching the fabric together around the seam to enclose the stuffing. Pin about ½ to ¾ inch in from the seam edge. Stop the piping short of the top and bottom corners, leaving about ½ inch on either end of the side seam with no stuffing. Repeat on the three other side seams. { *photo 2* }

8 Using embroidery floss or the equivalent, sew a rather broad running stitch (½-inch stitches work well) to enclose the stuffing in the edges. Make sure to enclose all the stuffing and sew tight to the edge of it so the piped edges are full enough to add structure to the piece. You can always add or subtract a little stuffing in this step to keep the piping width consistent.

9 Now pipe the top perimeter of the hassock. Start with your piping/stuffing at the halfway point on one of the sides. Work around the top edge, stuffing, pinching, and pinning. Pay special attention to getting plenty of stuffing into the corners above where the side-seam piping in step 7 ends. The corner may seem a bit tricky at first, but it takes its shape quite naturally as you work around it. Overlap the piping a little bit at the starting point so there is continuous piping all the way around with no breaks. Sew around the perimeter as described in step 8.

10 Now your hassock is finished, but empty. You can simply stuff it with loose polyfill stuffing–just stuff directly into the hassock cavity until it is full, taking extra care to fill all the corners. The overlap on the hassock bottom will be sufficient to keep all the stuffing in place. { *photo 3* } And you can always add more if the stuffing compresses over time. I like a little heavier, denser hassock, so I used a combination of polystyrene pellets (the beans in bean bag chairs) *and* polyfill. First I put the pellets into an old pillowcase and tied off the top to secure. I started by adding several handfuls of stuffing to the inside of the empty hassock, scrunching it toward the top. Then I put the pillowcase of pellets inside and added stuffing all around the sides of it, especially into the corners. I stuffed it pretty full, and it makes a pleasing resting spot for tired feet at the end of the day.

FELT BASKET

to CARRY & STORE

Modern life is full of things that need to be carried from place to place and stored away for safekeeping. This soft yet sturdy felt basket does that job with style. It's easy to make and the palette can be tweaked to match any décor.

MATERIALS	TOOLS	FABRICS
¼ yard each of gray, cream, and green natural-fiber felt heavyweight thread or embroidery floss	standard sewing basket { *see page 11* } a small plate to use as a circle template (about 8½ inches in diameter) **Template** page 122	**FOR THE BASKET:** Choose a natural fiber felt like a 100 percent wool or a wool blend (usually wool and rayon). Eco-felt (made from recycled plastic bottles) would work for this basket as well, although it has a tendency to pill. 

NOTES

Okay, full disclosure: This felt wonder makes a great sewing basket, too. In fact, the adorable thread caddy on page xx fits perfectly into this basket, and a pair of full-sized scissors and a measuring tape slip comfortably into the handle pocket. Of course the sewing kit (page 80) fits too, with room to spare for the various project pieces, making this a most efficient and useful accomplice for all your stitching escapades.

SIZE about 8 inches wide x 11 inches tall (including handles)

PORTABILITY FACTOR: { moderate }
A big, flat work space can be helpful as this basket takes shape.

photo 1

photo 2

photo 3

overstitching

1 Using the template on page 122, cut one 8½-inch circle from each of the three felt colors. Stack them together and sew around the perimeter about ¼ inch from the edge with an even running stitch. Trim ⅛ inch all around to even the edges of the basket bottom.

2 From each of the three felt colors, cut one strip 5 x 26 or 27 inches for the basket sides. Stack and sew them together as in step 1, but this time only on one edge of the strip. Trim as before.

3 Starting a few inches from the edge of the basket side strip, begin to pin it onto the basket bottom, lining up the edges as you go. Then sew the pieces together (six layers of felt!) using this row of stitches to cover or overstitch those from step 2. Work all the way around the circle and make a seam where one end of the basket side meets the other. If the fabric strip is a little long, cut it shorter. You want the side seam to be about ½ inch.
{ *photos 1 through 3* }

From each of the felt colors, cut two strips 21 x 3 inches for the straps. Stack and sew. { *photo 4* } Pin the strap along the side seam of the basket so one end of the strap is on one side of the seam and the other is on the opposite side of the seam. The strap should be on the outside of the basket and the ends of the strap should be even with the basket's bottom edge. Stitch down one side of the strap—overstitching the seam from before, then stitch across the bottom, and up the other side to attach the strap to the basket. { *photo 5* } Repeat on the other end of the strap. Don't sew the strap to the basket at the top edge of the basket. Leaving this open creates a pocket on the inside of your basket to hold things like scissors, small rulers, or knitting needles. Repeat for the strap on the opposite side of the basket.

Fold the strap in half at its top and sew through all six layers to make a thick and cushy handle. { *photo 6* } Note: This basket is best for carrying lightweight items.

photo 4

photo 5

photo 6

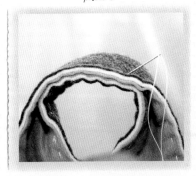

PRETTY PATCHES

of VINTAGE CALICO PRINTS

Mend your jeans and show your renegade craft style at the same time. A few charming scraps from your fabric stash and a couple of bold hand stitches makes even the most bedraggled old dungarees spanking new again.

MATERIALS	TOOLS	FABRICS
jeans to patch scraps of cotton print fabric iron-on denim patches thread for basting embroidery floss	standard sewing basket { *see page 11* } iron	**FOR THE PATCHES:** Raid your stash of vintage-printed cottons. Reproductions of feed-sack or Civil War era prints have built-in charm. Keep the palette simple and work off one or two base colors for a varied yet cohesive effect.

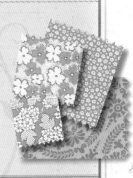

NOTES

I know, I know, holes in jeans are very fashionable right now. You can even buy brand-new jeans with the rips and tears and holes already made in them! However, this is a hip and charming way to buck that trend and make your jeans all your very own. Plus, they are so colorful and graphic, you can wear them with a plain sweater or T-shirt, and it's like having accessories built right in.

PORTABILITY FACTOR: { not so much }
Obviously, you won't be taking your iron to the cyber cafe so that half of this project needs to be done at home. But the stitching part is perfectly portable.

VARIATIONS on the THEME

Obviously, with something this cute you shouldn't stop at just your own jeans. This is a perfect way to patch up the battered knees and hole-y pockets of your kids' clothes.

Try other forms of embellishment like adding fabric to the inside of the waistband, putting a strip or a triangle of fabric over the edge of a pocket, adding some color to a cuff, or a strip to the zipper.

And don't think this only works with jeans—it's great for corduroys, khakis, even sweatpants.

1 Cut around the hole in your jeans to smooth the shape into a square, circle, or oval. Clip about ¼ inch into the corners of your square or at intervals around a circle. { *photo 1* }

2 Fold the edges of the hole back to the inside of the jeans and pin. Baste around the edges to hold. { *photo 2* }

3 Measure the hole and cut a piece of iron-on denim patch that is 1 to 2 inches larger than the hole in width and length. Next cut a piece of cotton print that is about ¾ to 1¼ inches larger than the hole in both dimensions. Center this cotton print on the adhesive side (wrong side) of the iron-on patch. Make sure there is at least ¼ inch border of iron-on adhesive exposed around the outside edge of the cotton piece. Put one pin in the center to hold. { *photo 3* }

4 On your ironing surface, fit the patch in the hole of the jeans with the right side of the cotton up and the iron-on adhesive face up on the inside of the jeans. Make sure to position it in the hole so all the raw edges of the cotton fabric are covered by the finished edge of the jeans. Remove the pin and follow the manufacturers directions to iron the patch into place. { *photo 4* } At this point, you will only be able to tack the patch in place as you will be ironing just on the front side. Remove the basting.

5 Thread a large, sharp needle with embroidery thread. Sew a line of running topstitch around the patch about ¹/₈ inch in from the edge of the hole. { *photo 5* } Add more rows of stitching if you wish.

6 Once the stitching is complete, turn the jeans inside out and finish ironing on the patch to secure it completely.

Running Topstitch

photo 1

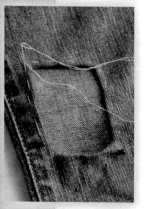

photo 2

photo 3

photo 4

photo 5

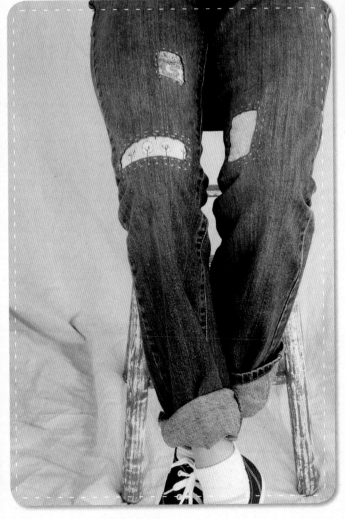

TEENY-WEENY BIKINI

all HAND STITCHED

All those yummy colors and cheerful patterns just make you want to smile. So put all that sunny spirit to good use on this sweet and sexy little bikini. No one will believe you sewed it by hand.

MATERIALS

½ yard of cotton print fabric, pre-shrunk

3-4 yards of fold-over elastic in a matching or contrasting color
or
3-4 yards of satin cord or ribbon for bikini straps and ties

1 yard of ¼-inch elastic

small scrap of soft cotton knit (you can use a piece from an old white t-shirt)

TOOLS

standard sewing basket
{ *see page 11* }

Template
page *124*

FABRICS

FOR THE SUIT: lightweight cotton in a fun, lively print. You can even consider mixing and matching prints to make a sort of "patch-work" bikini, so each side of the top is a different fabric, and the front and back of the bottoms are each unique.

NOTES

I made this suit using satin cord for the straps and ties on the bikini top. But if you like something a little wider and stretchier, the fold-over elastic works beautifully and requires less re-tying during a day in the sun. For the bottoms, I used fold-over elastic for the top edge and ties. Satin cord would work too, but the elastic makes a more sea-worthy suit.

SIZE Sizes S, M, L

PORTABILITY FACTOR: { very high }
Wouldn't this be the perfect thing to stitch on a day at the beach?

TEENY-WEENY BIKINI
all HAND STITCHED

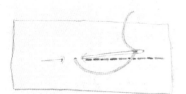

Backstitch

Tack Stitch

TO MAKE THE SWIMSUIT TOP:

1 Remember you can mix and match the sizes of top and bottom patterns you use to fit your own uniquely fabulous body. Cut out pattern pieces for the swimsuit top cups on page 124. Working first on the cleavage edge of the cup, fold the edge under 1/8 inch, then again 1/4 inch. Pin and stitch with a backstitch.

2 Working on the arm side edge of the cup, this time fold under 1/8 inch first, then 3/8 inch. This one is a little wider as it is the casing for the cord or elastic. This arm-side casing folds over the hem on the cleavage side at the top of the cup where the two meet. { *photo 1* }

3 Cut a piece of cord about 30 inches* (for fold-over elastic you'll need about 25 inches). Use a safety pin clipped to one end to feed the cord or elastic through the casing of the cup. Bring the end of the cord even with the bottom edge of the cup, and sew several stitches back and forth to secure the cord to the cup so it doesn't move. This will be the neckstrap of the bikini.

4 Next fold under the bottom edge of the cup, first 1/8 inch then 3/8 inch, to make a casing on the bottom of the cup. Stitch with a backstitch. Repeat steps 1–4 for the other cup.

5 Cut a piece of cord about 1½ yards long and use a safety pin to thread it through the cup casings. Start at the arm side of the right hand cup and exit the casing at the cleavage side. Then enter the cleavage side of the left hand cup, and exit through the arm side of the casing. Tie knots in the end of the cord or piping. Even out the cups so they are centered on the tie. Voila! You have just made a bathing suit top!

*Please test the cord or elastic length before cutting, so you can adjust it to fit your size as necessary.

photo 1

photo 2

TO MAKE THE SWIMSUIT BOTTOM:

7 Cut out pattern pieces for the bikini bottom on page 124-5 from the cotton print. Also cut out the lining for the crotch from the soft, light fabric.

8 Position the lining on the wrong side of the front piece of the bottom. Pin to hold. Fold under the top edge of the lining piece 1/4 inch, and sew it to the swimsuit front with tiny stitches.

9 Attach the front of the swimsuit bottom to the back using the French seam technique described on the next page.

10 Make the casings for the elastic at the leg opening by folding under the side edges 1/8 inch, then 3/8 inch. Sew with a backstitch. Repeat on the other side of the bottom. { *photo 3* }

photo 3

11 Cut a piece of 1/4-inch elastic about 12 inches long. Using a safety pin, thread it through the leg casing. Pin the elastic at both ends, and adjust the length. The elastic should be short enough so it causes the side to gather, but not so short that it causes the suit to pucker up into a little ball. Secure the elastic with several tack stitches about 3/4 inch in from either end. Cut off the excess elastic, leaving just about 1/8 to 1/4 inch beyond the tack stitches. { *photo 4* }

12 Fold the sides of the very top of the bikini bottoms in about 1/4 inch or so. Now create a casing on the top front edge of the suit by folding the edge under first 1/8 inch, then 3/8 inch. Pin and backstitch. Do a few extra stitches at each end of this seam to make the ends of casing extra secure as this is where the elastic tie will exit the suit. Repeat this on the back side of the suit bottom.

photo 4

13 Cut two pieces of fold-over elastic about 30 inches long. Use a safety pin to thread the elastic through the casing on the front of the suit bottoms. Center the elastic so there are equal length ties at both ends. Pull the elastic so that there is a nice amount of gather in the suit. Cut the ends of the elastic so there is about 6 to 10 inches on each side. Tie a knot in each end. Repeat on the back of the suit bottoms. Now tie the front ties to the back ties to bring the suit bottom together.

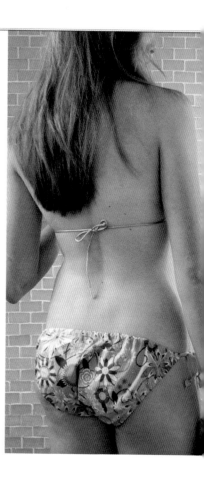

FRENCH SEAM (a beautifully finished edge)

A French seam is a way to create a seam that has no raw edges. We will use it here to attach the front of the bikini bottom to the back. Start by pinning the pieces together at the crotch with the wrong sides together. Stitch together with a backstitch about 1/4 inch in from the edge. Trim the seam to about 1/8 inch away from the stitching. Next turn the suit over and bring the seam together, this time with the right sides facing. Pin and sew in a little more than 1/4 inch so you are sure to encase the stitching from the earlier step. Now you have a seam that is tidy and finished both inside and out. How very French...

TEMPLATES

PERSONALIZED BIBS

from page 47

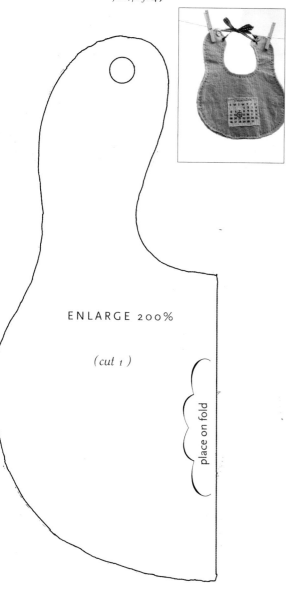

ENLARGE 200%

(cut 1)

place on fold

PILOT HAT

from page 63

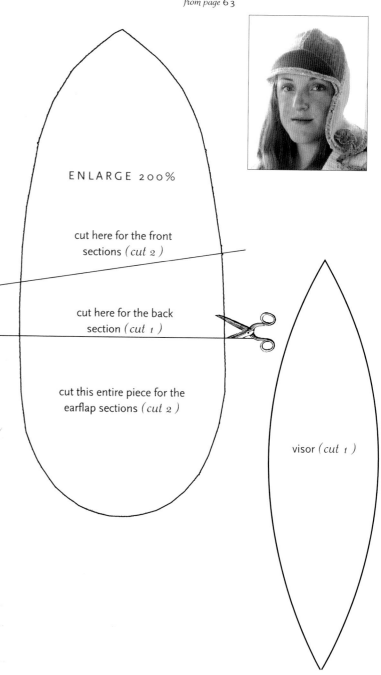

ENLARGE 200%

cut here for the front
sections *(cut 2)*

cut here for the back
section *(cut 1)*

cut this entire piece for the
earflap sections *(cut 2)*

visor *(cut 1)*

WOOL THROW

from page 59

ENLARGE 200%

ENLARGE 200%

THREAD CADDY and FELT BASKET

from page 29   *from page 107*

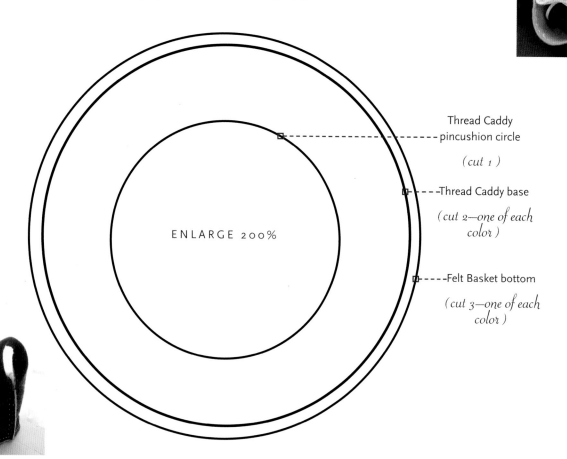

Thread Caddy
pincushion circle

(cut 1)

Thread Caddy base

*(cut 2—one of each
color)*

Felt Basket bottom

*(cut 3—one of each
color)*

ENLARGE 200%

BIG SOFT SPHERES

from page 25

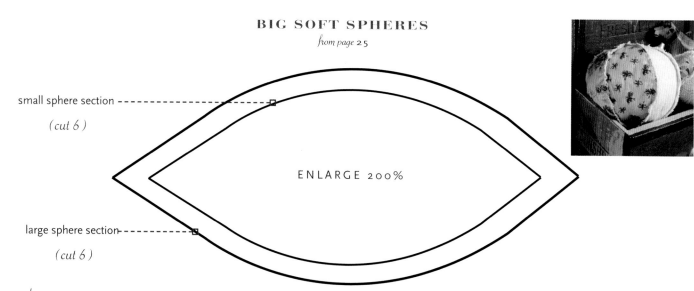

small sphere section

(cut 6)

large sphere section

(cut 6)

ENLARGE 200%

SWEET SLIPPERS

from page 67

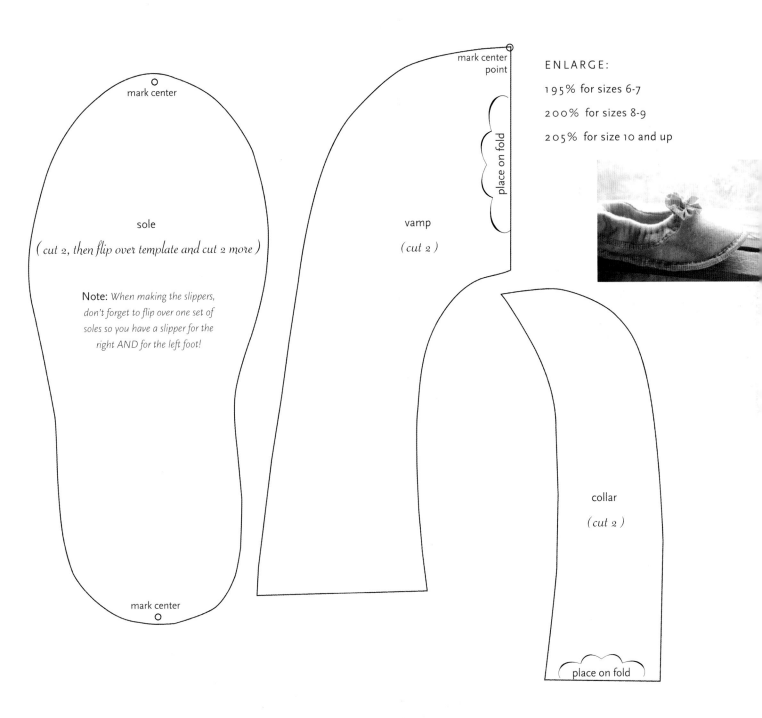

mark center

sole

(cut 2, then flip over template and cut 2 more)

Note: *When making the slippers, don't forget to flip over one set of soles so you have a slipper for the right AND for the left foot!*

mark center

mark center point

place on fold

vamp

(cut 2)

ENLARGE:

195% for sizes 6-7

200% for sizes 8-9

205% for size 10 and up

collar

(cut 2)

place on fold

TEENY-WEENY BIKINI

from page 115

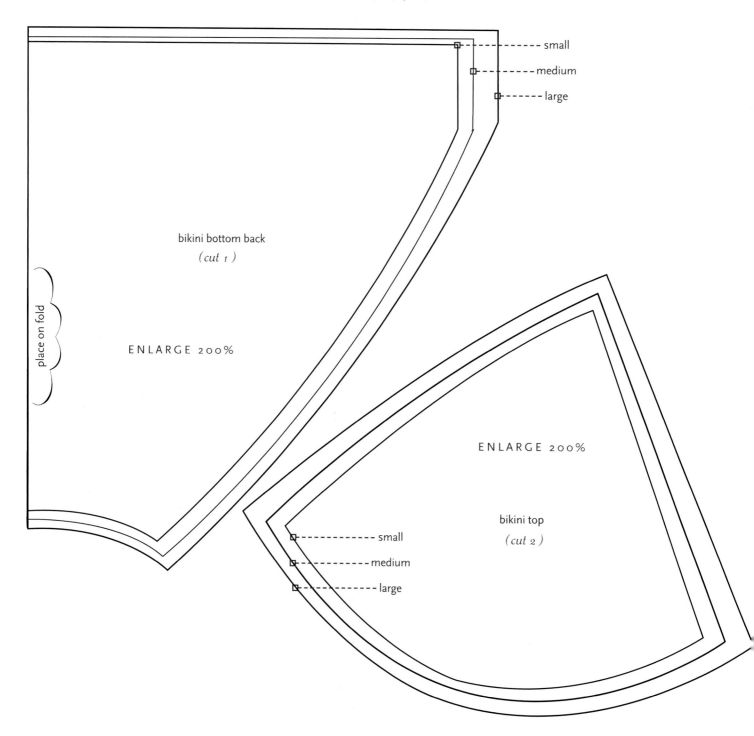

small

medium

large

bikini bottom back

(cut 1)

place on fold

ENLARGE 200%

ENLARGE 200%

bikini top

(cut 2)

small

medium

large

TEENY-WEENY BIKINI

from page 115

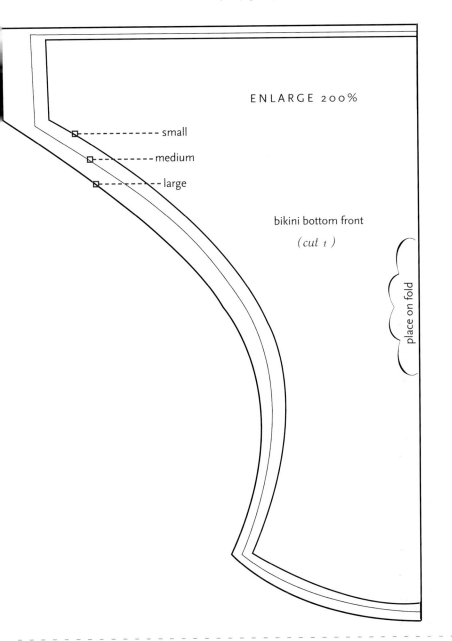

ENLARGE 200%

small

medium

large

bikini bottom front

(cut 1)

place on fold

ENLARGE
400%

bikini lining

(cut 1)

REVERSE APPLIQUÉ PILLOW   *from page* 72   cut along the black lines

SEWING KIT

from page 80

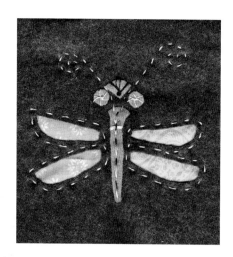

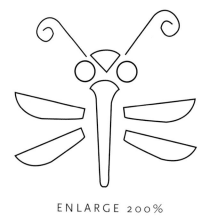

ENLARGE 200%

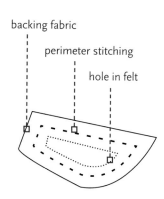

backing fabric

perimeter stitching

hole in felt

ENLARGE 200%

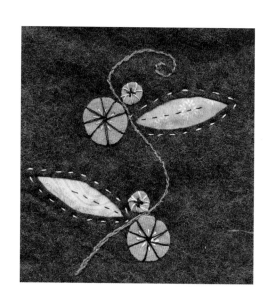

backing fabric - - - - - - - - - - - - - - - - -

perimeter stitching - - - - - - -

hole in felt - - - - - - - - - - -

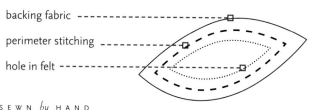

Acknowledgments

Who to thank for their gift of a lifetime's wisdom and practical knowledge? When I think about all the people who taught me how to stitch, or tuck, or knot, or pucker, my mind reels. I wonder who it was that first showed me how to squint at two fabrics to see if they looked good together? And who taught my fingertips to tell the difference between a scrumptious natural linen and a static-y, scratchy synthetic. Of course I know many of them, and can remember a few more (but what was my fifth grade home-ec teacher's name?). I have thanked her before, but must do it again and again and again—my grandmother Elizabeth Mader Abplanalp. She was the first to take my hands in hers and guide their purpose. She was fearless with a needle and thread, and full of the pithy wisdoms acquired in a lifetime of making things. She made a life full of reverence for the beauty and grace in simple, useful things. My mother, Marlies Harris—a wonderfully ambitious crafter herself—who graciously gave up her kitchen table (for days sometimes) to even my most outlandish crafting follies. To my husband Tom and my kids, Camille and Rainer for their usual elixir of patience and encouragement and cajoling and honest critique. And especially to Camille, for lending me her timeless beauty even on days when she didn't think she had any at all. To Margaret Willimann Blatter and Barbara Freigang Willimann for being my secret inspirations. To Isabelle Tierney for supplying a dose of passion and tenacity just when it was most needed. To Ambassador Deborah Jones for reminding me how far a woman can go and still be just the greatest girl. And of course, to Valerie Shrader at Lark Crafts who is a constant source of down-to-earth wisdom, technical expertise, and wry wit. Thanks for your infinite patience with my increasingly far-fetched excuses for missing deadlines. To Paige Gilchrist, who was my champion—and I suspect is a champion to just about everyone who knows her.

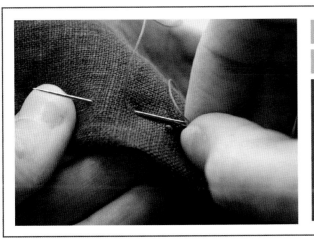

Index